T0360714

Reflections on Monetary Policy after 25 Years of the MPC

The Bank of England was given operational independence by the UK Parliament in 1997. The key feature of this independence is that the Bank's Monetary Policy Committee has sole responsibility for setting interest rates to achieve the government's inflation target. Featuring contributions from leading academics and practitioners, *Reflections on Monetary Policy after 25 Years of the MPC* assesses and reflects on this independence, particularly in relation to the activities of the Monetary Policy Committee. The book is organised around four main themes: the remit given to the Bank of England in 1997; the decision-making process by which the Bank determines monetary policy; the use of unconventional policy after the financial crisis of 2007–2011; and the scale and scope of the communication that the Bank uses to inform the public. It argues that the economy works best when agents understand why the central bank behaves in a particular way.

Sean Holly is Professor of Economics at the University of Cambridge and a Fellow of Fitzwilliam College, Cambridge. Among other books, he has published *Control, Expectations and Uncertainty* (with A Hughes Hallett), Cambridge University Press. One of his papers was in the top 10 papers, 2005–2015, published in the journal *Spatial Economic Analysis*. His research interests are in macroeconomics, monetary economics, applied econometrics and spatial analysis.

Michael McMahon is Professor of Macroeconomics at University of Oxford, Senior Research Fellow at St Hugh's College and CEPR research fellow. His interests are macroeconomics, monetary economics and economic data science. His economics education was from Trinity College Dublin (BA), and the London School of Economics (MSc, MRes, PhD).

Stephen Millard has a PhD from Northwestern University, where he studied with the late Nobel Laureate Dale Mortensen. He worked for many years on monetary policy issues at the Bank of England and has published extensively, including in the *Economic Journal* and the *Journal of the European Economic Association*.

Anna Watson is Peter Selman Fellow and Director of Studies in Economics at Fitzwilliam College, University of Cambridge. She was educated at the Warsaw School of Economics (MSc), University of Warwick (MSc) and University of Cambridge (PhD). Anna's research interests are in open-economy macroeconomics, monetary economics and international trade.

Macroeconomic Policy Making

Series editors:

Professor JAGJIT S. CHADHA NIESR
Professor SEAN HOLLY University of Cambridge

The 2007–10 financial crisis has asked some very hard questions of modern macroeconomics. The consensus that grew up during 'the Great Moderation' has proved to be an incomplete explanation of how to conduct monetary policy in the face of financial shocks. This series brings together leading macroeconomic researchers and central bank economists to analyse the tools and methods necessary to meet the challenges of the post-financial crisis world.

Published titles:

Chadha and Holly, *Interest Rates, Prices and Liquidity: Lessons from the Financial Crisis*

Coffman, Leonard and Neal, *Questioning Credible Commitment: Perspectives on the Rise of Financial Capitalism*

Chadha, Durré, Joyce and Sarno, *Developments in Macro-Finance Yield Curve Modelling*

Chadha et al., *The UK Economy in the Long Expansion and Its Aftermath*

Mizen, Rubio and Turner, *Macroprudential Policy and Practice*

Reflections on Monetary Policy after 25 Years of the MPC

Edited by

Sean Holly
University of Cambridge

Michael McMahon
University of Oxford

Stephen Millard
National Institute of Economic and Social Research

Anna Watson
University of Cambridge

CAMBRIDGE
UNIVERSITY PRESS

CAMBRIDGE
UNIVERSITY PRESS

Shaftesbury Road, Cambridge CB2 8EA, United Kingdom

One Liberty Plaza, 20th Floor, New York, NY 10006, USA

477 Williamstown Road, Port Melbourne, VIC 3207, Australia

314–321, 3rd Floor, Plot 3, Splendor Forum, Jasola District Centre, New Delhi – 110025, India

103 Penang Road, #05–06/07, Visioncrest Commercial, Singapore 238467

Cambridge University Press is part of Cambridge University Press & Assessment, a department of the University of Cambridge.

We share the University's mission to contribute to society through the pursuit of education, learning and research at the highest international levels of excellence.

www.cambridge.org
Information on this title: www.cambridge.org/9781009471879

DOI: 10.1017/9781009471886

First published 2024

A catalogue record for this publication is available from the British Library.

Library of Congress Cataloging-in-Publication Data
Names: Holly, Sean, editor.
Title: Reflections on monetary policy after 25 years of the MPC / edited by Sean Holly, University of Cambridge, Michael McMahon, University of Oxford, Stephen Millard, National Institute of Economic and Social Research, Anna Watson, University of Cambridge.
Description: Cambridge, United Kingdom ; New York, NY : Cambridge University Press, 2024. | Series: Macroeconomic policy making | Includes bibliographical references and index.
Identifiers: LCCN 2024020437 | ISBN 9781009471879 (hardback) | ISBN 9781009471862 (paperback) | ISBN 9781009471886 (ebook)
Subjects: LCSH: Bank of England. | Monetary policy – Great Britain. | Banks and banking, Central – Great Britain.
Classification: LCC HG939.5 .R44 2024 | DDC 332.4/491–dc23
LC record available at https://lccn.loc.gov/2024020437

ISBN 978-1-009-47187-9 Hardback

Contents

Figures

Tables

Contributors

WILLIAM A ALLEN (NIESR)

RICHARD BARWELL (BNPP AM)

BEN BROADBENT (Deputy Governor, Bank of England)

DAVID COBHAM (Heriot-Watt University)

MARIA DEMERTZIS (Deputy Director at Bruegel and part-time Professor of Economic Policy at the European University Institute)

PETRA GERAATS (University of Cambridge)

CHARLOTTA GROTH (Managing Director, Zurich Insurance Company Ltd)

SEAN HOLLY (University of Cambridge)

MERVYN KING (London School of Economics, former Governor of the Bank of England)

JENS LARSEN (Eurasia Group)

CATARINA MARTINS (Bruegel AISBL)

DELIA SIH CHIEN MACALUSO (University of Oxford)

MICHAEL MCMAHON (University of Oxford)

STEPHEN MILLARD (NIESR)

PAUL TUCKER (Harvard Kennedy School, former Deputy Governor of the Bank of England)

NICOLA VIEGI (University of Pretoria)

ANNA WATSON (Fitzwilliam College, University of Cambridge)

TONY YATES (Resolution Foundation)

I

Overview

1 An Introduction

Sean Holly, Michael McMahon, Stephen Millard and Anna Watson

The year 2022 marked 25 years since the Bank of England was given operational independence for the conduct of monetary policy. The aim of this monograph is to provide an overview of some of the key features of the UK's monetary policy framework during the last quarter of the century, their evolution over time as well as lessons learnt and the ways in which these lessons can inform the challenges ahead. The volume includes several chapters first presented at an MMF/NIESR workshop at Gresham College, London, in March 2022. It was then augmented by a special session at the Annual Conference of the Money, Macro and Finance Society at the University of Kent in September 2022, where both Mervyn King, a former Governor of the Bank, and Paul Tucker, a former Deputy Governor, provided their thoughts on the history and future of the Monetary Policy Committee (MPC). It was then enlarged further to provide a broader perspective by the addition of chapters commissioned later from Bill Allen, David Cobham and Petra Geraats.

The book is organised loosely around a number of themes – the scale and scope of the communication that the Bank uses to inform the public of its intentions; the objectives of the MPC and the Bank of England more widely, together with the tools needed to achieve these objectives, including the use of unconventional instruments in response to the effective lower bound to interest rates that appeared after the Global Financial Crisis (GFC); and, finally, the decision-making process by which the operationally independent bank decides on the monetary stance.

Before going on to these themes, the book starts with **Petra Geraats** providing an international perspective on MPC independence. The Bank was not the first to move to an inflation-targeting regime. New Zealand and then Canada were there first. Indeed, the adoption of inflation targeting in New Zealand was part of a greater reform to the conduct of public policy. The time of inflation targeting had come. Within two years it spread to Sweden, Australia and Spain, and by 2015 it had spread to almost 40 central banks.

When the operational independence of the Bank was announced by the new Labour government in 1997, this came as a complete surprise to the financial markets. Just as economic theory would suggest, an unanticipated switch to operational independence that was credible led to an immediate fall in long-term interest rates as expected inflation fell.

In the period after 1997, the Bank was widely regarded as a beacon for openness and transparency. According to the Eijffinger-Geraats index, in 1998 the Bank of England was ranked first on transparency among nine central banks. However, by the time the revised version of the index was published in 2022 (as the Dincer-Eichengreen-Geraats index) it suggested that the Bank had stagnated, while many other central banks had improved their transparency.

Geraats also dwells on the 2015 reforms to the communication of the Bank triggered by the Warsh Report. From a process of a drip feed of information, it went to a deluge when large amounts of news were provided on the same day (Super Thursday). This provides a good introduction to the first theme tackled in the book: central bank communication.

Transparency and Communication

In the original remit for the MPC in 1997 the Bank was made accountable to the government in the form of an open letter but also to the Houses of Parliament by appearing in front of select committees and to the public by means of the published minutes of MPC meetings and a regular *Inflation Report*. **Stephen Millard** puts this in the context of how the accountability of central banks changed radically from the end of the 1980s. Before 1989, the general practice was to regard monetary policy as a matter of private concern for wise central bankers. The more there was a 'monetary mystique' associated with the actions of central bankers the better.

But what was most striking about the adoption of inflation targeting in New Zealand was that the Governor of the Reserve Bank of New Zealand was obliged to communicate with the financial markets and the public. The main argument for imposing this was one of democratic accountability; in other words, voters had a right to know what their central bank was up to and why. But it could also be argued that monetary policy itself was more effective if *financial market participants* understood what central banks were up to and why as then financial markets would move in a predictable way for central banks. Inflation targeting with the corresponding need for public communication quickly spread to other central banks around the world. But it was not just the requirement for central banks to be democratically accountable. Open and transparent communication was a way of affecting expectations of future inflation. Anchoring inflation expectations became a cornerstone of the architecture of modern monetary policy.

Taking this idea further, central banks have increasingly adopted 'forward guidance' as a monetary policy tool. The idea is to communicate where interest rates are likely to move over the medium term. But, as **Ben Broadbent** reminds us, it is impossible to give markets any certainty as to the path of interest rates given the economy is constantly being buffeted by shocks. The best policymakers can do is to give statements about the path of interest rates conditional on other variables. At the same time, market practitioners need to remember that these statements are conditional and still adjust their expectations of future interest rates in response to economic shocks, rather than assume that such statements represent a firm commitment to the interest rate path.

But the success of central bank accountability depends critically upon how well communication works. How good have central banks been in communicating effectively? **Delia Sih Chien Macaluso and Michael McMahon** examine some recent evidence. It is clear that the formal adoption of inflation targeting helped reducing inflation expectations. However, it was only after the Bank gained operational independence in 1997, when expectations of inflation fell back close to the inflation target. This can be thought of as a low-frequency form of communication but with a higher frequency of communication with financial markets who take a more day-to-day interest in the plans and intentions of the Bank. However, the demands made on the style of communication changed over the 25 years. After the GFC of 2008, a loss of confidence in central banks changed the way in which the Bank communicated with the public as well as those in financial markets. Communicating directly with households became more important as they account for the majority of economic decisions. Then this quickly grew into a further need to educate households more in the terminology of economics that mattered for what the Bank does.

Objectives and Tools

The remit that the Bank was given by parliament was initially to pursue an inflation target of 2.5%, using the Retail Price Index (RPI) which excludes mortgage interest payments, with a margin of error of plus or minus 1 percentage point. In 2003 this was changed to a target of 2% based on the Consumer Price Index (CPI) but still with a margin of error of 1 percentage point. A value of inflation of 2% or thereabouts has turned out as the de facto target for most central banks around the world. However, there is a potential problem with a low inflation target because of the risk of hitting the effective lower bound of short-term nominal interest rates when monetary policy needs easing in response to a large negative shock. **Tony Yates** reviews the arguments for raising the inflation target. After explaining the origins of the now widely adopted 2% target for inflation, he provides an overview of the macroeconomic developments since the target's inception and the resulting challenges associated with the marked decline in interest rates after the GFC. The potential costs and benefits of changing the inflation target are then considered alongside alternative measures to address the problem of the lower bound.

There are many other features of the Bank remit that also deserve reconsideration. **Jens Larsen** draws attention to the apparent expansion of the remit of the MPC over time. In the original letter that the then Chancellor of the Exchequer wrote to the Bank in May 1997 the remit was very clear. Price stability is a precondition for high and stable levels of growth and employment. The monetary policy objective of the Bank is to deliver price stability and, without prejudice to this objective, to support the government's economic policy, including its objectives for growth and employment. The exceptional clarity and coherence of the remit were instrumental in providing a transparent accountability framework and a strong foundation for the new regime and the delegation of monetary policy to an independent central bank.

In 2013, following a major rethinking of the macroeconomic policy framework in the aftermath of the GFC, the remit was significantly expanded. In March 2021 the MPC's primary objective is still to stabilise the price level. However, the MPC now has more flexibility in dealing with inflation deviations from the target; more choice in terms of instruments; and a significant role in maintaining financial stability, even if it is secondary to the Financial Policy Committee (FPC). The government's economic policy objectives, which the MPC is obligated to support, are now also defined more broadly and include an extra commitment to achieving a net-zero economy.

Some may regret the loss of clarity of the remit: not only is it now too long and too complex for a non-technical audience to appreciate, but there is also a view that the expansion of the role of the MPC, and more generally of the Bank, poses substantial democratic challenges and ultimately threatens the Bank's independence and capacity to do well what only it can do: ensure price stability. However, there is also a strong argument for the remit to acknowledge the complex challenges faced by the macroeconomic policymakers today and to recognise explicitly the role that the MPC and the Bank now de facto play in the allocation of resources and the management of risk.

The global pandemic proved a particularly challenging time for monetary policymakers. **Charlotta Groth** argues that central banks were able to re-deploy the unconventional policy tools developed during the GFC but were also able to add new and even less conventional policies. This involved loosening policy aggressively and working with many different instruments simultaneously to maximise policy impact. One could argue that the episode has shown that monetary policy can also be effective in a low interest rate environment if central banks are willing and able to deploy multiple measures with scale and speed. But there are also several caveats. In particular, since the root cause of the lower bound on the interest rate is the issuance of paper currency, the development of Central Bank Digital Currency (CBDC) offers a potential solution to the problem and could allow for a return to more conventional monetary policy.

David Cobham links the development of these new tools to changes in the objectives of the Bank since the original remit given to the MPC in 1997. He notes that the MPC started out with one clear objective: price stability. At the same time, they had one instrument: the policy rate. Since then, the MPC has found itself being asked to consider other objectives including financial stability and output volatility. As a result, it needs additional instruments, in particular, quantitative easing (QE) – purchasing government bonds in exchange for a deposit at the central bank (expanding the balance sheet of the central bank), with the intention of lowering the longer end of the term structure – and macroprudential policy. (Although the FPC is charged with carrying out macroprudential policy, it does need to coordinate with the MPC.) He argues for some recasting of the role of the MPC and the way in which it operates. More specifically, he suggests that welfare might be improved if the MPC could adopt a broader set of goals while retaining the primacy of price stability: 'inflation targeting plus'.

When the Bank of England was first established at the end of the seventeenth century, its immediate purpose was to raise funds for the government. From its inception it therefore played a major role in government debt management. But the advent of QE has made this much more complicated. **Bill Allen** examines the complex relationship between monetary and debt management policies before and after the creation of the MPC, with a particular focus on the period of the Bank's operational independence. He shows how, during the last quarter of the century, the GFC and the resulting introduction of unconventional monetary policy tools have led to significant changes in the relationship between monetary policy and government debt management, which became much closer over time. While in the first decade of the MPC there was little need for coordination, with the adoption of QE, government debt management has been subordinated to monetary policy. This change has not only had a major impact on the conduct and effectiveness of monetary policy but has also led to a concerning shift in the maturity structure of the government's financial liabilities and has been associated with significant risks for both public finances and monetary policy objectives, which call for quantitative tightening (QT) as a matter of priority.

Decision-Making Process

The Bank has a specific remit from the government, with the MPC playing a key role in decision-making. The decision-making by committees is not identical. Broadly speaking, they fall into two categories: individualistic, where every member votes and these votes are then revealed; and collegial, where all members forge a consensus without attributing votes. The Bank of England and the Federal Reserve System are both prime examples of the former. The European Central Bank (ECB), by contrast, is a collegial-based system, where the decision reached is presented as that of the whole decision body. The emphasis is on communicating one view and therefore claiming ownership by all who participate.

Nevertheless, the individualistic approach might still offer the possibility of groupthink. **Richard Barwell** suggests that dissenting by only 25 basis points may be evidence that MPC do not in practice dissent enough. MPC members are individually and publicly accountable for their votes. Disagreement among the committee is inevitable; it is also desirable because it represents the individual judgements of members rather than an attempt to create a false consensus. It is a source of strength. MPC dissent is much more frequent than with other central banks and is not just token. It is argued that you get better decisions if you ask the nine people to say what they really think, instead of asking them to sit around and try and come to a consensus. Nevertheless, dissent seems to be rather limited, given that the many speeches given by MPC members suggest that there is significant disagreement on the economics of what the MPC is doing.

Mervyn King's contribution is from the perspective of someone who has voted at 194 meetings of the MPC. Moreover, as chief economist at the Bank from 1991 he presided over the publication of the Inflation Report in 1993 and the introduction of the fan chart in 1996. With the intellectual climate turning towards the importance of central bank independence, the Bank was quietly preparing itself for independence. Yet when operational independence was introduced in 1997 with the new Labour government, it was still a surprise to everyone. Over most of the 25 years the MPC has proved to be a success in achieving its target for inflation and in making the setting of interest rate a systematic and technical process rather than reflecting a political decision. Nevertheless, King believes that a mistake was made in 2020 and 2021, when – along with many other central banks – the Bank believed that the large fall in output resulting from the pandemic could predominantly be thought of as another form of a business cycle downturn that should be responded to by a major monetary impulse. But it was not a usual business cycle because potential supply had fallen as well.

The last contribution is by **Paul Tucker**, who retired as Deputy Governor of the Bank of England in 2013, had spent 33 years in total at the Bank, and served as a member of the MPC for 11 years. Tucker sets out a dozen propositions designed to underpin and, perhaps, revitalise the MPC and the monetary regime entrusted to it. Among other things, the propositions call for the reassertion of the primacy of the price stability objective, the clarification in legislation of the role of the lender of last resort facility and the simplification of the remit from the Treasury back to what it was in 2013. Tucker also urged a move back from the excesses of Super Thursday; provided an injunction on the members of the MPC to explain how exactly QE (and indeed QT) works in practice, to make a clear distinction between QE/QT and market making of last resort; and finally clarify how forward guidance works with a committee that decides policy by majority voting.

2 Twenty-Five Years of Bank of England Independence

An International Perspective

Petra Geraats

Introduction

The Bank of England gained operational independence in 1997. This chapter analyses and discusses how the Bank has operated and performed as an independent central bank. It combines a critical evaluation with useful lessons from an international perspective. The Bank's performance is compared with some of its peers, including the US Federal Reserve (Fed), the European Central Bank (ECB) and fellow inflation targeters. The chapter considers the Bank independence decision, the accountability, transparency and communications of its Monetary Policy Committee (MPC), its use of unconventional monetary policy and its inflation performance, before concluding.

Operational Independence

The decision to grant operational independence to the Bank in May 1997 was unusual for two reasons. First, it took place more than four years after the adoption of inflation targeting in October 1992.[1] Inflation targeting is usually associated with an institutional framework for monetary policy that features the 'trinity' of a mandate for price stability, central bank independence and accountability (Svensson, 2010). However, monetary policy decisions in the UK were made by the Chancellor of the Exchequer after consulting the Bank's Governor.[2] So, unlike other successful inflation targeters without formal independence (such as Norges Bank and until 1999 the Swedish Riksbank), the Bank of England lacked de facto instrument independence.

---

[1] The latter happened after a speculative attack on the British pound that caused the UK government to abandon fixed exchange rates as part of the European Monetary System on 16 September 1992.

[2] James (2020) provides a vivid, detailed description of monetary policymaking before the Bank of England's independence.

Second, the announcement by the new Chancellor of the Exchequer, Gordon Brown, on 6 May 1997 to give the Bank of England operational responsibility for setting monetary policy rates took many by surprise.[3] It happened only two business days after the UK general election, which 'New Labour' won by a landslide. Although its manifesto had pledged to reform the Bank of England to make monetary policymaking more 'free from short-term political manipulation', it had not committed to an independent Bank. Instead, Shadow Chancellor Gordon Brown had proposed a monetary committee with outside experts that would decide on the Bank's monetary policy advice to the Chancellor, which fell short of independence, but would be a useful stepping stone.[4]

So, Chancellor Gordon Brown's sudden decision to jump straight to operational independence for the Bank and make it effective immediately was in sharp contrast to central bank reforms in other countries, which usually take a long time to deliberate, decide and implement. As a result, the Bank independence event provides a unique 'natural experiment'.

The surprise announcement by Chancellor Gordon Brown on 6 May 1997 that monetary policy decisions from then on would be set by an independent MPC, consisting of nine members, including four external experts, had a dramatic effect on the yields on long-term UK government bonds ('gilts'). The 10-year gilt yield dropped by around 30 basis points (bp) and the 20-year gilt yield by 45 basis points that day,[5] reflecting a big drop in the long-term inflation compensation demanded by bond investors. Long-term 'break-even inflation' (the difference between yields on conventional and index-linked gilts based on Retail Price Index (RPI)), which had mostly been above 4% in the preceding years, fell around 50 bp following the surprise announcement of the Bank's independence,[6] and declined further towards 3% as the new MPC started operating, as shown in Figure 2.1.

As a result, the decision to give the Bank operational independence greatly reduced long-term inflation expectations/risks and made the 2.5%

---

[3] Although there had been a long drive for independence (see James, 2020, chapter 13), the final details were thrashed out and conveyed to the Bank over a bank holiday weekend, and announced without Cabinet discussion.

[4] The *Financial Times* called it 'Brown's half-way house for the Bank' (Münchau and Peston, 1997).

[5] At the very short end, interest rates actually rose (by 9 bp for the one-month nominal spot rate) as Brown had raised the Bank base rate by 25 bp to 6.25% that day before making the Bank of England independent.

[6] This effect increased in the term to maturity, so it was clearly attributable to the Bank's independence announcement rather than the 25 bp base rate rise. In fact, the instantaneous implied forward inflation rate in 5, 10 and 20 years declined by 32 bp, 46 bp and 53 bp, respectively, on 6 May 1997. Furthermore, the effect strengthened over time – the instantaneous implied forward inflation rate in 10 years averaged 2.7% in 1998 and 2.2% in 1999.

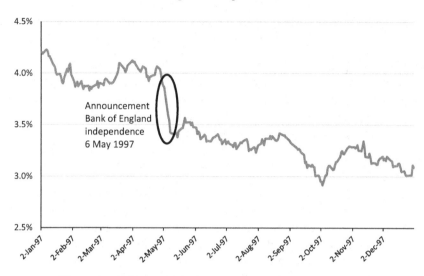

Figure 2.1 UK 10-year inflation compensation.
Note: UK 10-year break-even inflation (based on Retail Price Index),
2 January 1997 to 31 December 1997.
Source: Bank of England.

target for RPIX (Retail Price Index excluding mortgage interest payments)
inflation more credible, just as economic theory predicts.

MPC Accountability and Transparency

The delegation of monetary policymaking to an independent MPC was made
subject to transparency and accountability requirements to ensure democratic legitimacy. These are stipulated in the Bank of England Act of 1998,
which also enshrines price stability as the primary objective of monetary
policy. The Chancellor of the Exchequer sets the inflation target in an annual
remit letter for the MPC, which also asks the MPC to send an open letter if the
inflation target is missed by more than one percentage point, explaining the
reasons for the deviation and how the MPC plans to bring inflation back to
target. An explicit override mechanism allows the Treasury to give the Bank
directions on monetary policy if 'required in the public interest and by
extreme economic circumstances' and for at most three months,[7] but this
infringement upon independence has remained unused.

---

[7] Or for only 28 days if not approved by Parliament (Bank of England Act 1998, chapter 11,
part II, section 19).

The MPC is required to publish minutes of its meetings that include the individual voting records, and all MPC members are held accountable through regular appearances before the House of Commons Treasury Committee. Thus, accountability of individual monetary policymakers is stronger for the Bank of England than for the Fed and ECB.

In terms of monetary policy transparency,[8] the Bank has also done better than the Fed and ECB using the transparency index constructed by Eijffinger and Geraats (2006) – in fact, the Bank ranked first among nine major central banks in 1998. The Bank has been a leading example for macroeconomic transparency. It has published a very informative quarterly Inflation Report since 1993,[9] which was restructured and renamed Monetary Policy Report in November 2019. The Report presents the medium-term macroeconomic projections of the Bank and since August 1997 the MPC, including 'fan charts' for inflation, GDP growth (since November 1997) and the unemployment rate (since August 2013) that use confidence bands to convey uncertainty, a practice that has been adopted by many other inflation targeters.

Following the Bank of England forecasting review by Stockton (2012), the Report has included macroeconomic projections for a wider range of variables and greater detail about their underlying key judgements and risks, while the Bank's macroeconometric projection/policy models have been published since 1999. Further contributing to macroeconomic transparency, the Report has provided an annual discussion of the MPC's forecasting record since 1999. However, the last extensive evaluation of the MPC's forecasting performance dated back to November 2015 (BoE IEO, 2015) and was conducted by the Bank of England's Independent Evaluation Office (which was established in 2014). Since then the UK economy has experienced big structural changes due to Brexit and the Covid-19 pandemic and persistent, large overshooting of the inflation target, so an updated evaluation of MPC forecasts appeared overdue and should include the Bank's macroeconometric models, which has just been completed (Bernanke, 2024).

Although in the late 1990s the Bank was at the leading edge of monetary policy transparency together with the Reserve Bank of New Zealand, the modified and updated versions of the Eijffinger-Geraats index by Dincer, Eichengreen and Geraats (2019, 2022) indicate it subsequently stagnated, whereas most other central banks improved.[10] In particular, according to

---

[8] See Geraats (2014) for a review of theoretical literature and relevant empirical findings.

[9] Fracasso, Genberg and Wyplosz (2003) rated the Bank by far the best in their comprehensive evaluation of Inflation Reports for 20 inflation targeters, scoring over 9 out of 10 overall, while the average score was 6.5.

[10] The Reserve Bank of New Zealand is a notable exception; it changed from a single monetary policymaker to a monetary policy committee without releasing minutes or voting records, thus reducing procedural transparency.

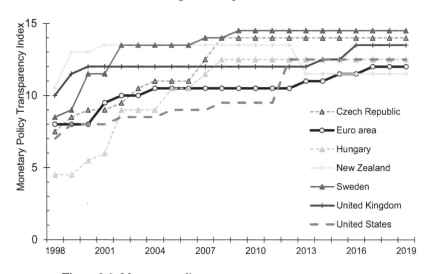

Figure 2.2 Monetary policy transparency.
Notes: Monetary policy transparency index (0–15) by Dincer, Eichengreen and Geraats (2022) for some top-ranking central banks from 1998 to 2019.

Dincer, Eichengreen and Geraats (2022), who rated the monetary policy transparency of 112 central banks from 1998 until 2019, the Bank has been overtaken by the Swedish Riksbank and Czech National Bank, who have been the two front runners since 2009, as shown in Figure 2.2. In the early 2010s, Hungary and Iceland (not shown) also scored higher than the Bank, and so did the Fed (2012–2013). But the Bank started catching up in 2014 and ranked third in 2019, closely followed by Chile and Norway (both not shown) and then Hungary and the US.

MPC Communications: From Drip Feed to Deluge

Although the Bank excelled in terms of macroeconomic transparency, it was rather opaque about its decision-making. Until July 2015, the MPC would just release a terse announcement of the monetary policy decision and only provide a prompt explanation when it adjusted policy settings. Once a quarter, the Inflation Report would be published about a week later, providing elaborate macroeconomic analysis and the MPC's medium-term macroeconomic projections. The minutes of the MPC meeting were released two weeks after the policy announcement,[11]

---

[11] Until October 1998, five weeks after the policy announcement, after the next monthly MPC meeting.

including the individual votes and a rather sanitised account of the policy discussion. As a result, there was a drip feed of key MPC communications spread out over two weeks: first the policy decision, usually without any explanation, then (once a quarter) the MPC projections and finally the voting record.

The Warsh (2014) review of Bank transparency recommended the adoption of international best practice by promptly releasing the monetary policy decision together with an explanation, the voting record and macroeconomic projections, with the minutes following a few weeks later. In response, the Bank decided to replace the drip feed with a deluge by releasing all this information at the same time, including the minutes and (once a quarter) the Inflation Report. This leaves financial markets and the press with a lot of material to digest very quickly, which is poor pedagogy, and makes it complicated to analyse the reasons behind market reactions.

Since it is not feasible to write and approve the minutes of the two-day MPC meeting overnight, the meeting is now spread out over seven days, with the main policy deliberation taking place a week before the policy announcement on Thursday. This makes it much more likely that there are significant news shocks during the intervening week, especially in times of turmoil, complicating the MPC's decision-making and communications.[12]

To allow the minutes to be finalised and approved for release at noon on Thursday, the MPC vote no longer takes place the morning of the monetary policy announcement, but generally the day before.[13] This appears to violate the transparency requirement in the Bank of England Act 1998 (chapter 11, part II, section 14) to publish the monetary policy decision 'as soon as reasonably practicable after each meeting of the Monetary Policy Committee'.[14]

Once a quarter the Bank has a press conference on the day of the monetary policy announcement at which the Governor presents the Inflation/Monetary Policy Report. However, that pales in comparison

---

[12] See Dincer, Eichengreen and Geraats (2019) for a further discussion and some examples. A more recent significant news shock was the announcement by the new Truss government of an Energy Price Guarantee (EPG) on 8 September 2022, the same day as the MPC's main policy deliberation. The death of Queen Elizabeth II later that day gave the MPC a convenient excuse to postpone the scheduled monetary policy announcement from 15 to 22 September 2022, allowing time to analyse the EPG's likely sizeable effects on inflation and get a staff briefing.

[13] There was even a two-day delay in 2020 when the decision to leave monetary policy settings unchanged made at the MPC meeting ending on 4 August was only announced on 6 August.

[14] The word 'reasonably' was added in an amendment by the Bank of England and Financial Services Act 2016.

with the ECB, which has held a press conference after each of its (scheduled) monetary policy meetings (held monthly until 2014), a practice the Fed has adopted since 2019.

The Bank has been an early adopter of the use of visualisations and non-technical explanations to make its communications more social media friendly and accessible to a wider audience. Since November 2017, the Bank has tried to convey the gist of its Inflation/Monetary Policy Report 'in a nutshell' through a few graphics with a terse text, and it also provides a non-technical summary with a few charts (initially labelled 'visual summary'). However, since July 2021, the ECB has provided a short accessible explanation in a visually more attractive way for every monetary policy decision ('our monetary policy statement at a glance'). So again, there is scope for improvements in MPC communications.

Achievement of Inflation Target

At first sight, the Bank has done impressively well in achieving its inflation target, with the 12-month Consumer Price Index (CPI) inflation averaging 2.0% during the 25 years after independence (from May 1997 until April 2022), seemingly right on target! However, the MPC had an inflation target of 2.5% in terms of RPIX until December 2003, after which it changed to 2% in terms of the CPI. When considering the deviation of the relevant inflation measure from the Bank's inflation target at the time (see Figure 2.3), UK inflation was on average 0.2 percentage points above target during the 25 years after independence, rising to 0.4 percentage points when including all of 2022.[15]

During the decade between the Global Financial Crisis (GFC) and the Covid-19 pandemic, from January 2010 until December 2019, average UK CPI inflation was also above target at 2.2%. In contrast, as shown in Table 2.1, average US CPI inflation was 1.8% during that decade, and using the Fed's preferred measure, PCE[16] inflation averaged only 1.6%, clearly below the Fed's longer-run inflation goal of 2%.[17] Average Euro Area inflation using the Harmonized Index of Consumer Prices (HICP) was only 1.4% during the 2010s, falling well short of the ECB's medium-term inflation objective of 'below, but close to' 2% at the time.

---

[15] Although RPIX inflation averaged 2.4% from May 1997 until December 2003, slightly below the 2.5% target, CPI inflation averaged 2.3% (2.6%) from January 2004 until April (December) 2022, clearly above the 2% target.

[16] Personal Consumption Expenditures Price Index.

[17] The latter is in terms of PCE inflation and was first announced by the Federal Reserve (2012).

Table 2.1 *Average inflation in UK, US and Euro Area, 2010–2019.*

Average 12-month inflation, 2010–2019	Measure	Inflation	Core inflation
United Kingdom	CPI	2.2%	2.1%
United States	CPI	1.8%	1.8%
	PCE	1.6%	1.6%
Eurozone	HICP	1.4%	1.1%

Notes: Consumer Price Index for all urban consumers for US and HICP for eurozone. Personal Consumption Expenditures (PCE) price index is seasonally adjusted. Core inflation excludes energy and food, and for UK also alcoholic beverages and tobacco. Sample period: January 2010 to December 2019. Source: ONS, Federal Reserve Economic Data (FRED), ECB Statistical Data Warehouse and author's calculations.

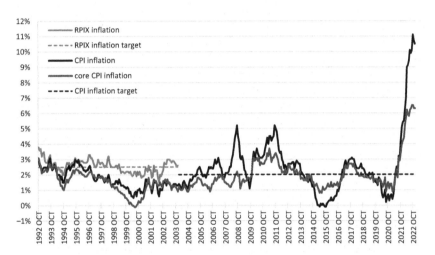

Figure 2.3 Bank of England inflation target achievement.
Note: UK 12-month inflation and inflation targets, from October 1992 to December 2003, for RPIX, and for CPI until December 2022. Core CPI inflation excludes energy, food, alcoholic beverages and tobacco. Source: Office for National Statistics (ONS) and Bank of England.

However, inflation could deviate from its target due to unanticipated food and energy price shocks, so it is better to evaluate a central bank's performance using 'core' inflation, which excludes food and energy (and in the UK also alcoholic beverages and tobacco). Using core inflation measures (see Table 2.1), the ECB performed even worse with an average of 1.1% during the 2010s, the Fed the same with an average of 1.8% and 1.6% for core CPI and PCE inflation, respectively, but the Bank performed closer to its target with an average of 2.1%. Partly due to a Brexit-related inflation surge,[18] the UK avoided inflation averaging significantly below target during the 2010s. This helps to explain why, unlike the Fed and ECB,[19] the Bank did not feel the need to conduct a wide-ranging review of its monetary policy strategy.

Unconventional Monetary Policy

During the GFC triggered by the collapse of Lehman Brothers in September 2008, the Bank reduced its main monetary policy instrument, Bank Rate, to a then historic low of 0.5% and followed the Fed by adopting 'unconventional' monetary policy through outright large-scale asset purchases (LSAPs). Whereas the Fed had started 'credit easing' in late 2008,[20] the Bank embarked on 'quantitative easing' (QE) on 5 March 2009 when it announced £75 billion of asset purchases of mainly UK government bonds ('gilts') to be completed over three months. The latter was also unusual because the Bank had been very reluctant to give any indication about future monetary policy actions for its monthly Bank Rate decisions.

For its subsequent rounds of QE (amounting to a total of £895 billion by December 2021),[21] the Bank stuck with this practice of announcing a specific, large (target) amount of bond purchases to be completed over multiple months,[22] rather than a fixed amount per month lasting for a flexible, indefinite period, like the Fed and ECB.[23] Announcing a specific amount of QE upfront provides clarity about the stimulus,

---

[18] Although UK CPI inflation was significantly below target from mid-2014 until end-2016, even languishing close to 0% (with core inflation around 1%) during 2015, the large depreciation of the British pound due to the Brexit referendum on 23 June 2016 was followed by a big rise in CPI inflation of 2.5 percentage points during the subsequent 15 months, with CPI (core) inflation staying close to 3% (2.7%) for half a year (see Figure 2.3).

[19] See Federal Reserve (2020) and European Central Bank (2021) for further details.

[20] The Fed's 'credit easing' started with the announcement of the purchase of $500 billion agency mortgage-backed securities and $100 billion agency debt on 25 November 2008.

[21] Total asset purchases of gilts (+ sterling non-financial investment-grade corporate bonds) amounted to £200 billion for QE1 (March 2009 to February 2010), £175 billion for QE2 (October 2011 to October 2012), £60 billion (+£10 billion) following the Brexit referendum (August 2016 to February 2017) and £440 billion (+£10 billion) during the Covid-19 pandemic (March 2020 to December 2021).

[22] The amount of gilt purchases each time ranged from £50 billion to £200 billion, and the completion periods lasted around 3 or 4 months for QE1 and QE2, 6 months after Brexit and 6 or 12 months during the Covid-19 pandemic.

[23] Such 'QE infinity' was introduced by the Fed in September 2012 (lasting until October 2014 after 'tapering'), adopted by the ECB for its Asset Purchase Programme

which could make it more effective, but also more difficult to curtail as that could be interpreted as 'reneging' on the QE announcement.[24]

In addition to LSAPs, the Bank also introduced special schemes to stimulate bank lending, including the Funding for Lending Scheme (FLS, in July 2012) and the Term Funding Scheme (TFS) with additional incentives for lending to SMEs (TFSME, in March 2020). The latter was a targeted version of the TFS that was introduced in August 2016 to reinforce the pass through of the August 2016 cut in Bank Rate to 0.25% following the Brexit referendum of 23 June 2016. Bank Rate reached a new historic low of 0.10% after an unscheduled MPC meeting on 19 March 2020 due to the Covid-19 pandemic.

In contrast to the ECB, Danish Nationalbank, Swedish Riksbank, Swiss National Bank and Bank of Japan, the Bank of England did not adopt negative interest rates. However, in February 2021 the Bank started technical preparations to add a negative Bank Rate to its monetary policy toolkit, which was completed in August 2021. Some MPC members had advocated using it, which was helpful in providing stimulus – even without implementing it, this actually reduced short-term interest rates to negative levels.[25]

The Bank was slow to adopt explicit forward policy guidance.[26] It took a change of Governor (from Mervyn King to Mark Carney) for the Bank to provide explicit guidance on Bank Rate. On 7 August 2013, the Bank announced state-contingent threshold guidance that it did not intend to tighten policy at least until the unemployment rate had fallen to 7%, which was expected to take at least two years based on the MPC's projection. But market participants foresaw a much faster decline, leading to less stimulus than intended, and the threshold was reached in about two quarters. Subsequently, the MPC has made intermittent use of explicit forward guidance.

In response to the Covid-19 pandemic, the MPC introduced state-contingent fuzzy threshold guidance in August 2020 that it did 'not intend to tighten monetary policy at least until there is clear evidence that significant progress is being made in eliminating spare capacity and achieving the 2% inflation target sustainably'. These conditions are quite vague and open to different interpretations, making it hard to judge

---

that started in 2015, and again used by the Fed during the Covid-19 pandemic (but the ECB's Pandemic Emergency Purchase Programme was completely flexible).

[24] Two MPC members who initially voted against Brexit QE did not vote against its continuation 'given the potential costs to the economy of reversing the programme underway', as noted in the December 2016 minutes.

[25] Short-term nominal spot rates were negative for several months, with 6–12 month rates −0.15% in late 2020.

[26] See Geraats (2014) for a review of forward policy guidance.

whether there was clear evidence of them. This guidance remained in place until August 2021, when it was modified to 'some modest tightening of monetary policy' was likely necessary, and one MPC member voted to discontinue gilt LSAPs due to rising inflation.

Post-pandemic Inflation Surge

UK 'core' CPI inflation (excluding energy, food, alcohol and tobacco) had been significantly below 2% during the first year of the Covid-19 pandemic (even dipping below 1%), but it returned to around 2% mid-2021, and then started to increase rapidly. In August 2021, CPI and core inflation both rose above 3%, requiring an open letter to explain the target deviation. The MPC attributed most of this to 'base effects' after low inflation a year ago and there was large uncertainty how the end of the furlough scheme end-September would affect the unemployment rate. The majority of the MPC appeared to attach greater weight to the latter instead of the MPC's primary objective of price stability, voting in September 2021 to maintain Bank Rate at its historic low of 0.1% and to complete £200 billion QE announced in November 2020 as planned (by end 2021). But two MPC members voted against the latter, and the MPC strengthened its forward guidance of 'some modest tightening'.

With CPI and core inflation still close to 3% in September 2021, a rate rise was widely expected following statements by MPC members (including Governor Andrew Bailey). However, the majority of the MPC again preferred to wait for uncertainty to resolve and voted to maintain policy settings on 4 November 2021.[27] Three MPC members dissented and voted to discontinue gilt LSAPs, and two voted to raise Bank Rate to 0.25%. Forward guidance became stronger, indicating it was likely 'necessary over coming months to increase Bank Rate'.

In November 2021, CPI (core) inflation reached 5% (4%), again triggering an open explanatory letter. Meanwhile, the Omicron Covid-19 variant emerged, which appeared to be much more transmissible than the dominant Delta variant, so many considered an upcoming rate hike unlikely. Nevertheless, the MPC finally raised Bank Rate to 0.25% in December 2021, just when QE was completed. However, MPC communications had managed to wrong-foot markets in two consecutive meetings.

At the next MPC meeting in early February 2022, Bank Rate was raised by 25 bp to 0.50%, but four out of nine MPC members dissented in favour of a 50 bp hike. In addition, the MPC voted to start 'quantitative

---

[27] The two-year gilt yield dropped 21 bp that day as the anticipated rate rise failed to materialize.

tightening' (QT) and reduce its £895 billion stock of bond purchases by ceasing to reinvest maturing bonds. So, less than two months after completing QE, the Bank started QT – a remarkable U-turn.

In spring 2022, core inflation stabilised around 6%, while CPI inflation surged to around 9%. The Russian invasion of Ukraine in February 2022 caused a large increase in energy and food prices, with CPI inflation reaching 10% in July 2022 and even 11.1% in October 2022.[28]

The MPC had announced that active QT would start in October, but it had to postpone its gilts sales (by one month) due to the fallout of Chancellor Kwasi Kwarteng's 'mini-Budget' on 23 September 2022[29] and even engage in LSAPs of long-term gilts for financial stability purposes, while still doing passive QT. So the Bank's price and financial stability policies clashed.

Conclusions

The sudden and swiftly executed decision to grant operational independence to the Bank of England in May 1997 provides a unique natural experiment that shows the sizeable benefits of moving monetary policy-making from elected politicians to an independent MPC with experts. Long-term government bond yields and long-term inflation compensation fell by around 50 basis points after the announcement, showing improved credibility of the inflation target.

The newly independent Bank of England has become one of the world's leading central banks in terms of monetary policy transparency. It has excelled in macroeconomic transparency, but it has long displayed weaknesses in policy transparency and still faces considerable challenges with its communications.

Unlike some of its peers, the Bank did not significantly undershoot its inflation target on average during the decade following the GFC, but this may be due to the inflationary effects of the sharp depreciation of the British pound following the Brexit referendum.

The Bank's routine use of big multi-month QE announcements and its fuzzy state-contingent forward guidance during the Covid-19 pandemic may have made it more reluctant to curtail QE and start raising the policy rate. Moreover, the MPC appears to have lost sight of its primary objective of price stability with core inflation far above the inflation target. The

---

[28] The Energy Price Guarantee announced by the Truss government helped to reduce the rise in inflation.

[29] Besides a very large energy support package, it included large unfunded permanent tax cuts, while sidelining the Office for Budget Responsibility (OBR).

post-pandemic inflation surge is putting the effectiveness of the Bank's monetary policy framework to the test.

References

BoE IEO (2015), *Evaluating Forecast Performance*, Independent Evaluation Office, Bank of England.

Bernanke, Ben (2024), *Forecasting for monetary policy making and communication at the Bank of England: a review*, Bank of England.

Dincer, Nergiz, Barry Eichengreen and Petra Geraats (2019), 'Transparency of monetary policy in the postcrisis world', in David Mayes, Pierre Siklos and Jan-Egbert Sturm (eds.), *The Oxford Handbook of the Economics of Central Banking*, chapter 10, 287–334, Oxford University Press.

Dincer, Nergiz, Barry Eichengreen and Petra Geraats (2022), 'Trends in monetary policy transparency: Further updates', *International Journal of Central Banking*. 18(1), 331–48.

Eijffinger, Sylvester, and Petra Geraats (2006) 'How transparent are central banks?', *European Journal of Political Economy*. 22(1), 1–21.

European Central Bank (2021), *Strategy Review*, 8 July. www.ecb.europa.eu/home/search/review/html/index.en.html.

Federal Reserve (2020), 'Review of monetary policy strategy, tools and communications', 27 August. www.federalreserve.gov/monetarypolicy/review-of-monetary-policy-strategy-tools-and-communications.htm.

Federal Reserve (2012), 'Federal Reserve issues FOMC statement of longer-run goals and policy strategy', Federal Reserve press release, 25 January. www.federalreserve.gov/newsevents/pressreleases/monetary20120125c.htm.

Fracasso, Andrea, Hans Genberg and Charles Wyplosz (2003), 'How do central banks write? An evaluation of inflation targeting central banks', Geneva Reports on the World Economy, Special Report 2, International Centre for Monetary and Banking Studies and Centre for Economic Policy Research.

James, Harold (2020), *Making a Modern Central Bank: The Bank of England 1979–2003*. Cambridge University Press.

Geraats, Petra (2014), 'Monetary policy transparency', in Jens Forssbæck and Lars Oxelheim (eds.), *The Oxford Handbook of Economic and Institutional Transparency*, chapter 3, 68–97, Oxford University Press.

Münchau, Wolfgang, and Robert Peston (1997), 'Brown's half-way house for the Bank', *Financial Times*, 27 February, page 8.

Stockton, David (2012), 'Review of the monetary policy committee's forecasting capability'. Report presented to the court of the Bank of England, October. www.bankofengland.co.uk/-/media/boe/files/news/2012/november/the-mpcs-forecasting-capability.pdf.

Svensson, Lars E. O. (2010), 'Inflation targeting', in Benjamin M. Friedman and Michael Woodford (eds.), *Handbook of Monetary Economics*, Volume 3, chapter 22, 1237–302, Elsevier.

Warsh, Kevin (2014), *Transparency and the Bank of England's Monetary Policy Committee*. Bank of England. https://www.bankofengland.co.uk/-/media/boe/files/news/2014/december/transparency-and-the-boes-mpc-review-by-kevin-warsh.pdf.

II

Communication

3 Reliable Partners

Ben Broadbent [1]

It was a pleasure to deliver the speech that became this chapter at Gresham College, a place that has held public lectures on important societal questions for over four hundred years. That makes it one of the few City institutions that's been around longer than the Bank of England. I would also like to thank both National Institute of Economic and Social Research (NIESR) and the Money, Macro and Finance Society (MMF) for putting together this volume. Over the years the work of both institutions has been invaluable to the UK policy community.

We are living through the most extraordinary – and in many ways extraordinarily unwelcome – time. Russia's unprovoked attack on Ukraine has brought war to Europe for the first time in decades, with all its terrible humanitarian consequences.

From an economic perspective, coming on top of what was already a very steep rise in the cost of globally traded goods, in the wake of the pandemic, the invasion has led to substantial rises in the cost of energy and other commodities. As a big net importer of manufactures and commodities it's doubtful that the UK has ever experienced an external hit to real national income on this scale. From the narrow perspective of monetary policy it will result in the near term in the difficult combination of even higher inflation but weaker domestic demand and output growth.

However, the Monetary Policy Committee (MPC) has already said quite a bit about these things, individually and collectively, and – dramatic though its economic effects have been – my topic today is not this awful conflict or the immediate questions it poses to monetary policy. Instead, I wanted to talk about something more general, namely the communication

[1] I've received helpful comments from colleagues at the Bank of England. I'd like to thank Jack Meaning, Alberto Polo and Tuli Saha for their help in preparing this chapter. Particular thanks are due to Fabrizio Cadamagnani and Rich Harrison, who ran the simulations for Figures 3.4–3.6 and wrote the appendix. The views expressed are my own and do not necessarily reflect those of the Bank of England or other members of the Financial Policy Committee or the Monetary Policy Committee.

of monetary policy, and specifically the role of 'forward guidance'. I will take this to mean statements by monetary authorities about future policy.

The question 'What's going to happen to interest rates?' is asked of us routinely. (Sometimes it's phrased directly, sometimes more circuitously, but it always seems to come in one form or another.) And perhaps it's understandable that people should want to know, particularly in an environment as uncertain as this. If it were possible to eliminate or reduce at least one source of unpredictability, wouldn't that be a good thing? And since the MPC is in control of interest rates why can't it just tell us what it's going to do?

The problem is that we can't be sure. Interest rates are not an end in themselves. They're a means of meeting our objectives: the stabilisation of inflation over the medium term and, subject to that, the stabilisation of economic activity. And because there are lots of unpredictable shocks hitting the economy, things that would otherwise (and often do) move output and inflation around, the appropriate path of interest rates is necessarily unpredictable as well. The skipper of a boat, adapting to a skittish wind, and interested in making the journey as smooth as possible, may have perfect control of the tiller. But that doesn't mean she can tell you exactly which position it will be in at every point in the future. That will depend on the direction of the wind at the time.

It's not that monetary authorities are unconcerned about expectations of future interest rates. Quite the opposite: these expectations are central to the transmission of policy. We directly determine only one particular – and very short-term – interest rate (what commercial banks get paid on their overnight deposits, or 'reserves', at the central bank). But demand and spending depend more on longer-term interest rates. In the UK, around half of corporate borrowing has a maturity of three years or more. Some mortgages have interest costs tied directly to Bank Rate, but most are now fixed for at least two years. And these longer-term rates depend in their turn on expectations of how the short-term interest rate evolves over the future. So they matter.

Equally, however, these expectations should – and generally do – respond to the news about the economy of their own accord, without the need for any explicit prompting by the central bank. The private sector forms its own views about how the economy might evolve over the future, views that are continually adjusted as new information comes in. As long as people also understand the objectives of the central bank, and therefore the appropriate response of policy, they should then be able to work out for themselves what that news means for the likely path of interest rates.

Sometimes, when economic conditions are relatively stable, there isn't that much to work out, as one can observe the central bank's 'reaction function' – how it responds to incoming data – pretty much directly. In the years prior to the Global Financial Crisis (GFC), official interest rates in the UK were very tightly correlated with economic activity (and exhibited very little dependence on anything else).

Figure 3.1 is one way of representing that relationship: it plots the change in the average interest-rate vote on the MPC, in basis points, against a survey-based measure of economic growth.[2] At least until 2008 the correspondence was extremely tight. From an economic perspective, the behaviour of policy over that period was understandable. If you think trend supply growth is pretty stable – and that was generally the view at the time – then stronger activity will always mean more pressure on resources, weaker activity less of it. So, to stabilise inflation, your best response is to lean against these swings in demand. If, in addition, there are few other enduring influences on inflation (from the rest of the world, for example) then there's no reason to respond to anything else.

Whatever the rationale, this stable 'reaction function' made it easier for asset prices to respond as well in a similar fashion. Figure 3.2 plots that

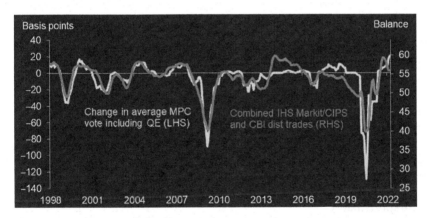

Figure 3.1 Monetary policy and economic activity tightly correlated before the financial crisis.
Six-month rolling averages. Combined IHS Markit/CIPS and CBI distributive trades lagged one month.
Sources: ONS, IHS Markit/CIPS, CBI, Bank of England and Bank calculations.

[2] I've chosen the former because it's smoother than the actual interest rate and the latter because it's a monthly rather than quarterly series.

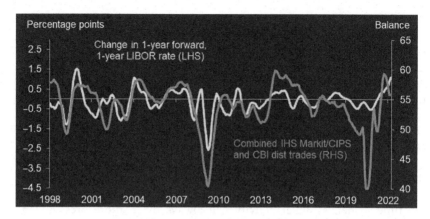

Figure 3.2 Forward interest rates and economic activity also co-moved closely before the financial crisis, less so afterwards.
Six-month rolling averages. Combined IHS Markit/CIPS and CBI distributive trades lagged one month.
Six-month change in one-year forward one-year LIBOR rate, spliced onto one-year, one-year OIS rate in 2022.
Sources: ONS, IHS Markit/CIPS, CBI, Bloomberg Finance L.P. and Bank calculations.

same survey-based measure of economic growth against expected future interest rates (specifically the three-year forward rate). Even without any verbal encouragement from the MPC, monetary conditions tightened in response to stronger growth. As Mervyn King pointed out at the time, the cyclicality of forward interest rates, in anticipation of action by the MPC, itself helped to stabilise demand, putting less burden on the policy rate. (Some of you may remember that, in an unlikely comparison, he suggested this was similar to the behaviour of the hapless England defenders against the great Diego Maradona in the 1986 World Cup. This was the first, and I daresay the last, time that MPC members were likened to an elite sportsman.)[3]

So if financial markets are able to react this way, without any explicit hints from the policymaker, why has there since been more communication from central banks about future policy – and more expectation of it in financial markets? What is the rationale for 'forward guidance'?

At least in theory there are two distinct types of guidance. The reasons for both, I think, are connected with changes in the economy in recent years. But they are quite distinct, and it's important to understand how.

---

[3] King (2005).

The first – sometimes described in the economics literature (somewhat grandiosely) as 'Delphic' guidance – seeks in general to convey what is sometimes referred to as 'private information' held by the central bank. This makes it sound more exciting than it really is. More often than not it means making clear to the outside world the policymaker's view of how the economy might evolve over the future – its forecasts – and to clarify the so-called 'reaction function' (how monetary policy might respond to possible future events).

I said the simple pre-crisis pattern in Figure 3.1 was the appropriate way to set interest rates if you're in an environment where swings in economic growth are driven predominantly by shocks to demand, things that push output and inflation in the same direction, and if there are few other enduring shocks to inflation. But if that was a reasonable view of the world in the years before the financial crisis – a period some now call 'the Great Moderation' – it's clearly been much less of one since. Productivity growth is less predictable and it's harder to count on a single rate of 'trend growth'. (Nor can we be assured of a fixed, 'neutral' rate of interest, below which policy is necessarily expansionary and contractionary only above it. In particular, it became clear even before the crisis, and increasingly so after it, that this 'neutral rate' had over many years been declining.) And if we'd forgotten during the Great Moderation that domestic output isn't the only thing that affects inflation we've certainly been reminded of it since. In the UK, the two big exchange-rate depreciations in 2008 and 2016 pushed up inflation for a protracted period, independently of activity at home. The strains in global goods markets caused by the pandemic, and the substantial impact on commodity prices of Russia's invasion of Ukraine, have done the same, to an even greater extent. In this environment, simple rules of thumb like Figure 3.1 are less reliable – you can see clearly how the correlation between the two lines declined after the crisis – and it might therefore be an advantage for the central bank to communicate more about how policy is being set.

This 'Delphic' guidance can come in various forms. Regular forecasts are part of it. You can speak directly about the changing environment and the implications for the reaction function, perhaps with the aid of particular simulations (I gave a talk in 2013 arguing that, when productivity growth is less predictable, the monetary authority will want to put less weight on output and more on the domestic labour market[4]). Monetary authorities have often made more specific remarks about the near-term path of interest rates, depending on how things turn out ('if the economy develops in line with our forecast then policy might be expected to do

----

[4] Broadbent (2013).

such-and-such' is a typical example). A handful of central banks publish forecasts of the policy rate, alongside those for GDP and inflation. Their joint behaviour can help people understand how these things interact.

It's worth noting up front that not all forms of 'Delphic' guidance have to involve direct communication about the future path of interest rates. And, whatever its precise form, the important point about this sort of guidance is that it's always conditional. These are – and should always be seen as – 'if ... then' statements. Their purpose is not to pledge some particular path of policy, independently of what happens to the economy. It's to help people understand the dependence of policy on the economic outlook.

The other form of guidance – sometimes called 'Odyssean' – is quite different in this respect. It actively promises a certain path – in particular to keep interest rates very low – almost regardless of how things turn out. It's a means of easing monetary conditions, and specifically of lowering longer-term real interest rates, when the outlook for inflation is weak but the immediate policy rate is constrained by the lower bound (and if other alternatives like quantitative easing (QE) are for some reason unavailable or ineffective). If you're able to convince people that, even in the event of a positive shock to inflation in the future, you won't raise interest rates, this can push up expected inflation, thereby reducing the real forward rate of interest and encouraging more demand today. This 'promise to be irresponsible'[5] won't necessarily be believed because, when the time comes, and if there were subsequently some significant rise in inflationary pressure, the policymaker will be tempted to go back on the earlier promise and respond by raising interest rates. The optimal policy is intrinsically 'time inconsistent'. But if you can find a way of tying yourself to the policy in advance – like Odysseus lashing himself to the mast of his ship – then this is in principle an effective way of easing monetary conditions, even when the policy rate itself can't be lowered any further.

It's striking that this 'Odyssean' guidance has received much more attention in the economics literature – but, in the real world, and despite often being right up against the lower bound, central banks have used it only rarely. This may be because, in practice, it's quite difficult to make credible commitments of this sort (and because central banks have also been able to use QE).

Whatever the reason, most 'forward guidance' has been of the 'Delphic', more conditional form.

Yet my impression is that outside observers can sometimes mistake one for the other: the 'if' clause is forgotten, or downplayed, and purely

---

[5] See Krugman (1999).

conditional statements somehow get interpreted (or rather misinterpreted) as hard commitments.

It's not entirely clear why this is the case. It may be quite a deep-seated tendency. Some psychological research demonstrates that people can misconstrue 'if... then' statements, particularly if they're fairly abstract. It may also be wishful: because people don't like uncertainty and would therefore prefer there to be some fixed path of interest rates set in advance, perhaps they're prone to believe that this is what they're being told.

But there's no doubt it happens. In September 2013, the MPC said that a minimum necessary condition for a rise in interest rates was that unemployment should fall below 7%. This was not a sufficient condition, and the Committee was also at pains to emphasise that the actual path of rates would depend on the outlook for the economy at the time. Yet quite a few observers viewed the condition as a hard trigger and were confused when rates didn't immediately and automatically rise in response (memorably, one MP subsequently likened the Committee to 'an unreliable boyfriend, blowing hot and cold').

Similarly, in a speech in July 2015,[6] the then Governor Mark Carney said the 'the decision as to when to [start raising interest rates] will likely come into sharper relief around the turn of the year'. This was no more than suggestive and was immediately qualified with a remark about the importance of economic developments in the interim:

> I am conscious of several important considerations which mean the actual path [of interest rates] almost certainly will not be mechanical, linear or pre-determined. First and foremost, shocks to the economy could easily adjust the timing and magnitude of interest rate increases .... There is, in fact, a wide distribution of possible outcomes around any expected path for Bank Rate, reflecting the inevitability that the economy will be buffeted by shocks and that monetary policy will have to adjust accordingly.

Yet when – thanks precisely to such shocks – interest rates did not subsequently rise 'around the turn of the year', he was criticised for having misled people.

Such criticisms, whether justified or not, are par for the course and may not be that consequential in the grand scheme of things. But there could be a more material cost if, in mistaking conditional for unconditional statements, people come to rely on them at the expense of thinking about the economy, and its implications for interest rates, for themselves. As I said earlier, it's an important part of the transmission of policy, and of the stability of demand more generally, that prices in financial markets respond to

---

[6] Carney (2015), 'From Lincoln to Lothbury: Magna Carta and the Bank of England', speech given at Lincoln Cathedral as part of the Lincoln Lectures 2015, 16 July.

economic news as it comes in, without the need for any prompting by the central bank. That is precisely the purpose of the 'Delphic' sort of guidance that, in the main, central banks have employed. But as Figure 3.3 demonstrates, the sensitivity of market interest rates to releases of economic data seems to have declined somewhat in recent years.

There could, of course, be several explanations for this. It may well be that, precisely because the economy seems less predictable than it was during the 'Great Moderation', markets are understandably more reluctant to infer things about the medium term from shorter-term data. The fact that central banks have for so long been pressed up against the lower bound would also naturally have attenuated the reaction of forward rates to news about the economy (they can't fall as far as they usually would in response to negative news). But it's possible that an over-reliance on central bank communication, and a misinterpretation of it as a fixed plan for interest rates, has contributed to this as well. If you believe that the monetary authority will always tell you in advance what it's going to do you may feel less inclined to anticipate and price such a response yourself.[7]

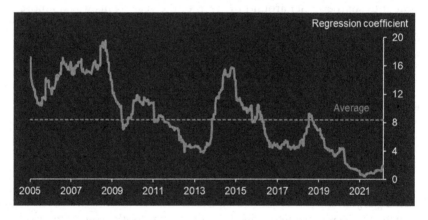

Figure 3.3 The sensitivity of market interest rates to news in economic data has fallen in recent years.
Sensitivity of three-year spot rates to economic data news: coefficient in regressions of change in the interest rate to change in a data surprise index prepared by Bank staff, using 12-month rolling windows.
Sources: Bloomberg Finance L.P., Refinitiv Datascope and Bank calculations.

---

[7] On this point see also Feroli et al. (2017) and Swanson and Williams (2014).

I don't know if this is true. It's really no more than a conjecture and a relatively idle one at that. But it would be an irony if an effort to get people to think more about how monetary policy might respond to events, by communicating something akin to a 'reaction function', had actually had the opposite effect.

At any rate, having already gone through at some length the point I want to make, the rest just fills in some gaps. I'll start with a more formal description of 'Odyssean' guidance, explaining why, when the interest rate is up against the lower bound, there could be very significant gains to credible commitments to keep rates low in future – but also why, in practice, such credibility is hard to secure.

There's then a brief discussion of various forms of guidance in the real world. As we'll see, the distinction between 'Odyssean' and 'Delphic' guidance is less clear in practice than in theory. In the real world the dividing line between them is sometimes a bit fuzzy. This may have contributed to the conflation of the two – more exactly the (mis)interpretation of conditional as unconditional statements – in the outside world. But I think it's clear enough that central banks have rarely, if ever, committed themselves unconditionally to future policy.

It's clear too that, on several occasions, the outside world has nonetheless viewed these statements as promises. I'll give some examples before a short concluding section.

Credible, 'Low-for-Long' Guidance as a Means of Easing Policy at the Lower Bound

So let's start with the value of commitment when the policy rate is close to the lower bound. As you know, the last thirty years have seen a marked decline, around the world, in the underlying, 'equilibrium' real rate of interest (sometimes called 'R*'). This is a real phenomenon, not a monetary one, caused by some combination of a greater desire to save – across the world as a whole – and weaker investment demand. But central banks have still had to accommodate the decline, and the appropriate nominal rate of interest has therefore fallen alongside this 'R*'.[8]

However, there's a limit to how far the nominal rate can fall. As long as people also have access to physical cash, bearing zero interest, it's not possible to lower the official rate much below that level. And when the

---

[8] Remember that the nominal rate of interest is the real rate plus expected inflation (π^e). So the 'neutral' nominal rate is something like $i^* = R^* + \pi^e$. Broadly speaking, policy will be contractionary (expansionary) if the official interest rate is higher (lower) than i^*.

'normal' policy rate is already close to that lower bound there's very little room for conventional policy to respond to negative, disinflationary shocks. This in turn creates the potential for deflationary traps. Because the policy rate can't fall in response, a decline in inflation expectations pushes up real interest rates and depresses demand and inflation, and this justifies the original (and self-perpetuating) weakness of expectations.

These traps are potentially very costly as they can lead to protracted periods of unnecessarily weak economic activity. It was in a determined effort to avoid them, having already cut interest rates as far as they could, that central banks then turned to alternative, 'unconventional' monetary policies. For the most part this meant QE. Asset purchases are designed to keep a lid on forward rates, thereby supporting demand and activity.

In the academic literature, however, many economists argued for an alternative – and potentially more powerful – option, namely a committed form of forward guidance. The economist Michael Woodford has been one prominent advocate.[9]

Remember that the name of the game, when faced with this risk, and having run out of room to cut the policy rate any further, is to lower forward real interest rates. In this respect, a credible declaration that you will keep the actual policy rate low, even in the event of a future increase in inflation, does two things. It keeps nominal forward rates low. It also raises expected inflation. In the normal course of events the central bank would tighten policy as inflation rises, choking it off before it turns into a persistent overshoot. If you tell people you're not going to do this then – as long as they believe you – this will push up inflation expectations and further depress the real rate of interest.

In many simple economic models expected real interest rates have almost as big an effect on spending as the current real rate. In that setting, credible guidance that depresses those forward real rates can therefore be an effective way of boosting demand and combatting the risk of deflation. Figure 3.4, based on simulations with a simple (and pretty standard) model of the economy, gets the point across.

What we've done is to hit this simple model economy[10] with lots of simulated shocks and measure how far it is, on average, from meeting the central bank's objectives – keeping inflation close to target and output close to potential. A simple measure of this, based on a 'loss function' that weights together the variances of the output gap and inflation, is plotted

---

[9] Woodford and others have argued that QE works mostly because it signals something about future interest rates. See, for example, Woodford (2012). For an overview of the transmission channels of QE see Broadbent (2017) and Bailey et al. (2020).

[10] There's a formal description of the model, and how Figures 3.4–3.6 were generated, in the appendix.

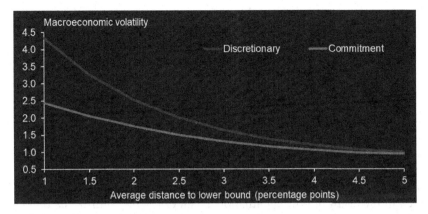

Figure 3.4 The ability to commit credibly to future policy helps soften the effects of the lower bound.

on the y-axis. Note that the perfect score of zero isn't attainable. Because there are so-called 'trade-off-inducing' shocks in the model, things that push the objectives in different directions, inflation and demand can't both be perfectly stabilised.[11]

We've plotted this performance while varying two key things. One is the distance between the 'neutral' nominal rate of interest and the lower bound. This is plotted on the x-axis. The larger this gap (i.e. the further you are to the right), the less the lower bound is likely to matter. There may occasionally be shocks that are bad enough to take you there, but they obviously become rarer the more distant the average policy rate is from its floor. Maybe you can think of this a reasonable description of the 1990s (when the neutral interest rate was comfortably above zero and 'forward guidance' was no more than a twinkle in Michael Woodford's eye).

The second is the scope for this committed ('Odyssean') form of guidance. QE isn't available to either of the policymakers in Figure 3.4. But one, at least, has the capacity to commit credibly to particular policies beyond the current date. The average loss in this case is plotted in the line marked 'commitment'. The other policymaker can't do this. He takes the lower bound into account when setting current policy, but, unfettered by any sort of prior commitment, he's free to reset policy each period as he sees fit.

This may sound like a good thing (isn't it better always to have full discretion?) and there are certainly many instances in which the

---

[11] In this simple model, monetary policy affects inflation pretty much immediately. In the real world it takes time. Lags between policy and its effects are another reason why perfect stabilisation isn't possible.

'committed' policymaker would prefer to be released from his earlier promise. But perhaps a better way to think of it is to recognise that, thanks to this ability to make credible commitments, he essentially gets to choose future as well as current policy. This is a pretty valuable addition to the set of monetary tools when the current interest rate can't be cut (and if the economy responds sensitively to forward rates).

Without it, as you can see, the simulated performance of the economy deteriorates significantly as the neutral real interest rate gets closer to the lower bound. Unable to do much about them, the fully discretionary policymaker will spend quite a bit of time in these low-inflation, low-output traps. But because he effectively controls future as well as current policy and can credibly 'promise to be irresponsible' (i.e. to keep rates low even in the event of positive inflationary shocks in the future), the other policymaker manages to avoid the worst effects of the lower bound for interest rates.

Forward Guidance in Practice

What about the real world? In practice, looking at what central banks have actually said about future policy, the boundary between the two is less clear in practice than in the theory. Even a fully discretionary policy-maker – one who can't credibly commit to future policy decisions – may react slightly differently to incoming data around the lower bound. As I pointed out in the introduction, there may be other changes in the economy (less predictable productivity growth, for example) that also warrant a change in the 'reaction function'. So, if a statement signals some shift in how policy might respond to the economy, that doesn't necessarily make it 'Odyssean'.

Nor does commitment mean you ignore entirely what's going on in the economy: the committed policymaker is still 'data dependent' in some sense, just less so – less responsive to inflation overshoots in particular – than the discretionary policymaker. So although I've been stressing the contingent nature of 'Delphic' guidance, and the relative invariance in the case of commitment, it's not a rigid distinction. In any case, perhaps there's always some room for interpretation when it comes to language.

That said, I think one can still outline some broad parameters – things that colour a statement more in one shade than another – that can help distinguish the two. For example, Odyssean, committed guidance is probably more likely to refer to dates – a time frame for low interest rates – than to economic conditions alone. If it does tie future policy to economic variables it may explicitly pick out inflation expectations (as Odyssean guidance is explicitly designed to raise them). More generally, it will actively seek to convey a more dovish stance relative to incoming data. Without these things, a statement that simply says 'We expect such-and-such a policy to be appropriate given the current outlook' doesn't seem to me to qualify, especially if it goes on to stress the dependence of one on the other. The same goes for forecasts of future interest rates based on the latest projections for the economy. These are just an effort to explain more about the 'reaction function'.

On these grounds, and even with a fairly liberal interpretation of these requirements, it's difficult to pick out many episodes that clearly count as pre-commitment. Perhaps the US Fed's communications during and in the years after the financial crisis came the closest, though the shift to more Odyssean-like guidance was as much evolutionary as revolutionary.

The Federal Open Market Committee (FOMC) had begun to signal the likelihood of a long period of low interest rates as early as December 2008, though to begin with, this was phrased simply as what would be justified by the economic outlook: 'Weak economic conditions are likely to warrant exceptionally low levels of the federal funds rate for some time.'

The following summer, the statement still explained the outlook for policy as a normal and justifiable response to that for the economy but, for the first time, introduced specific timelines: 'The Committee currently anticipates that economic conditions ... are likely to warrant exceptionally low levels for the federal funds rate at least through mid-2013.'

Some years later, by 2012, the FOMC was indicating not only a time horizon for low rates but had added two important extra ingredients – first, the recognition that policy was 'highly accommodative' and second, that it would remain so even after a fuller economic recovery had taken hold: 'The Committee expects that a highly accommodative stance of monetary policy will remain appropriate for a considerable time after the economic recovery strengthens. [It] ... currently anticipates that exceptionally low levels for the federal funds rate are likely to be warranted at least through mid-2015.'

I suppose you could still quibble about how committed this language really is. But the clear dovish skew puts it more firmly in the Odyssean camp than the earlier statements. This is also the view of Del Negro and co-authors, looking at the effects of this guidance.[12] In any event, to my mind it's hard to find guidance from other central banks that has come as close as this. If you squint a bit you could perhaps see some of the same in the European Central Bank's new strategy, published last autumn. The ECB said that, when rates were close to the lower bound, policy should

---

[12] Del Negro, Giannone and Patterson (2023).

respond 'forcefully and persistently' and that '[t]his may also imply a transitory period in which inflation is moderately above target'.[13]

But this is about the ECB's general strategy, not a particular path for policy. Even a discretionary policymaker would in practice recognise that the proximity of the lower bound can affect appropriate policy. And the ECB took pains to say that, although the approach might skew the subsequent distribution of possible inflation outcomes to the upside, this would be 'accidental not deliberate'. So I don't think it really qualifies.

Anyhow, these episodes aside, most guidance seems to me to be pretty clearly 'Delphic' in nature: it's about the central bank's view of the economic outlook (a forecast) and about policy conditional on it (a 'reaction function'). As a general matter, we know that's the purpose of numerical forecasts for interest rates because those central banks that publish them tell us so. The Norwegian central bank, for example, describes the rationale like this: 'With the aid of the policy rate paths and related communication, Norges Bank provides forward guidance regarding future policy rate developments and information about the central bank's response pattern.'[14]

As for the UK, the few times the MPC has issued formal guidance about policy, it's very clearly of this type. If ever it's said something about future policy, it's always been in the context of, and dependent on, the outlook for the economy and inflation at the time.

In August 2013, the MPC said it would not raise interest rates 'at least' until unemployment had fallen to below 7% (so passing this threshold was a necessary but not a sufficient condition for a hike). It added the proviso that low rates would be maintained only 'provided this does not entail material risks to either price stability or to financial stability'.

My own interpretation was that this guidance helped to signal the greater dependence of policy on the labour market at a time of greater uncertainty about supply. Whatever one's view, it's clear, I think, that this was not designed to engineer above-target inflation – nor was 7% unemployment a hard trigger for a rate rise (it was only a necessary pre-condition).

---

[13] Lagarde (2021). Press conference on the ECB monetary policy statement on 22 July 2021.

[14] Norges Bank's monetary policy handbook (2022). Other examples are from the Riksbank: 'The publication of repo rate forecasts has given the general public greater insight into monetary policy and improved possibilities for evaluation and accountability' ('The Riksbank's experiences of publishing repo rate forecasts', 2017), and from the Reserve Bank of New Zealand: 'Published forecasts help markets assess the economic environment and understand our policy strategy', McDermot (2013).

In February 2014, the Committee commented about future policy in the context of a low 'neutral' rate of interest. While the MPC would always in practice do what was necessary to keep inflation stable over the medium term, it was unlikely that this would require interest rates to rise to levels seen in the first few years of inflation targeting (let alone the 1970s and 1980s). What might then have counted as a 'loose' level of interest rates could now be 'tight'.

However, we were conscious of the risk that people might see this as some sort of commitment to keep interest rates low, come what may – it wasn't that – and therefore added that, whatever one's expectations, actual policy would depend on the economic outlook at the time:

The actual path Bank Rate will follow over the next few years is, however, uncertain and will depend on economic circumstances. Bank Rate may rise more slowly than expected, and increases in Bank Rate may be reversed, if economic headwinds intensify or the recovery falters.

Similarly, Bank Rate may be increased more rapidly than anticipated if economic developments raise the outlook for inflation significantly.

Later on, in the summer of 2015, we described guidance about future interest rates, more succinctly, as 'an expectation, not a promise'.

The Time Inconsistency of Optimal Policy: Why 'Low-for-Long' Guidance May Not Be as Powerful as Simple Models Predict

So why, in view of the power of the policy apparent in Figure 3.4, hasn't this committed form of guidance been used more often?

In their 2023 paper, Del Negro and co-authors claim that, while it had helped ease monetary conditions, the Fed's post-crisis guidance had had significantly less impact on demand and inflation than predicted by theory. Their explanation was that, in the real world, demand is less sensitive to forward interest rates than the theory presumes. That's probably true. Certainly the very simplest models, in which a drop in forward rates five years ahead (say) does almost as much to stimulate spending as a same-sized cut in the current rate, surely exaggerates the impact.

But there may also be a more fundamental problem with the policy. It's intrinsically 'time inconsistent' (to use the technical term). From today's perspective, in the face of a risk of deflation, it would be better if you could persuade people that you will keep policy loose for an extended period, even in the event that inflation rises above target. But you know full well – as does the private sector – that, when the time comes, you'll want to do something else in that case. It's one thing to promise in abstract to be 'irresponsible', in advance of some hypothetical inflationary shock. It's quite another, in the teeth of a real one, actually to be irresponsible. By that time the promise is in the past, the inflation is happening now, and it obviously feels more important to deal with what's in front of you than to abide by a pledge you might have given some time – even some years – earlier. Knowing this, people will naturally be sceptical about the promise in the first place and the policy would lose its force.[15] You'd be back in the world of the 'discretionary' line in Figure 3.4 (subject to the effects of QE).

In a paper in 2019,[16] economists at the Bank formalised this idea by introducing a probability that the central bank reneges on earlier commitments. The probability was assumed to rise in line with the scale of the subsequent inflation (and therefore the temptation to abandon the promise). But it's precisely from the possibility of these high-inflation states of the world that the prior commitment really gains its force. (This is the Catch-22 of time-inconsistent policies: the only promise worth making is one you'll subsequently be tempted to break.) So even a relatively small effect of this sort can have a material impact on the credibility, and therefore the power, of the guidance (the dotted line in Figure 3.5). The line marked 'commitment' presumes that there's some mechanism – some Odyssean mast to which you could tie yourself – ensuring that the cost of breaking the promise is always greater than the temptation to do so.

In practice, it's hard to see that there is one. The importance of maintaining reputation obviously helps. There's a cost to breaking one's word. But that might not be enough, especially if your promise seeks to constrain not just your future self but your successor as well. That obstacle is all the greater if, as in the UK, policy decisions are made not by collective consensus but by democratic vote. Each member of the MPC is individually accountable for his or her vote. It's part of the UK's constitution that 'no Parliament can bind its successor'.[17] I'm not sure it would cut much ice with parliament's Treasury Committee if I said I was voting not on the basis of what was going on in the economy right now but instead because of some guidance a few years ago by an earlier MPC.

---

[15] In a speech in 2012, while still governor of the Bank of Canada, Mark Carney, put this well: 'Today, to achieve a better path for the economy over time, a central bank may need to commit credibly to maintaining highly accommodative policy even after the economy and, potentially, inflation picks up. Market participants may doubt the willingness of an inflation-targeting central bank to respect this commitment if inflation goes temporarily above target. These doubts reduce the effective stimulus of the commitment and delay the recovery.'

[16] Haberis, Harrison and Waldron (2019).

[17] More formal, written constitutions, which usually can't be altered except by super majorities in the legislature and therefore evolve more slowly than the electoral cycle, could be seen as a commitment device to allow for (otherwise) time-inconsistent but optimal government policies.

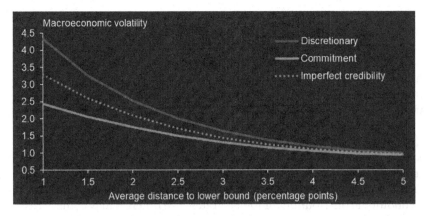

Figure 3.5 Commitment policy loses much of its power if it isn't fully credible.

The Interpretation of Guidance and the Potential Costs of Mistaking the Conditional as Unconditional

I picked out a moment ago a couple of key bits of guidance by the MPC. There were several others. But all of them contained the message that the outlook for interest rates would be dependent on that for the economy and inflation at the time.

However, I think it's clear from the reaction to these episodes that the points we were trying to get across – including this critical point about conditionality – were not universally understood.

One particular problem was that, in response to the September 2013 guidance, many commentators appeared to see the 7% unemployment threshold as a sufficient, not just a necessary, condition for the tightening policy. We would apparently be 'forced' to raise interest rates if unemployment fell below this level, whatever the outlook for inflation at the time.

As for the general point about conditionality, it was only two days after the February 2014 Inflation Report that the BBC said: 'What is forward guidance? It is making a promise about the future, particularly about future interest rates.'[18] And despite the intervening (and frequently reiterated) point that our statements about future policy were 'an expectation, not a promise', a newspaper comment, published as recently as 2022, referred to the 'many promises [made by the MPC] to raise interest rates'.

---

[18] See Miles (2014).

There may be several reasons for this. One must be the very fact that there are these two distinct forms of communication – one much closer to a 'promise' than the other – yet economists use the word 'guidance' for both, distinguishing them only with the (slightly arcane) classical descriptors 'Delphic' and 'Odyssean'. This kind of jargon can obscure more than it clarifies, and one can quite understand why people might muddle them up.[19]

More generally, it's possible that central banks probably don't help themselves with language which, while it may seem clear to people whose job it is to think about these things, is unclear or ambiguous to others. To the economist author the meaning of a phrase 'we expect the appropriate level of interest rates to be X' may be 'X is the arithmetic mean of a conditional distribution for interest rates'. To others it may come across simply as 'interest rates will be X'. In hindsight, the logical structure of the MPC's 2013 guidance linking policy to the rate of unemployment – 'if not p then not q' – may well have been too convoluted to be readily understood. There is psychological research in the field of cognition, demonstrating that people have an easier time understanding conditional statements if they're less abstract and more rooted in real-world experience.

In addition, I suspect there may be sometimes a degree of wishfulness involved. None of us likes uncertainty. Long-standing research has identified related, and deep-seated, cognitive biases. We are all prone to over-confidence in our own predictions and, after the event, to the belief that what has happened was entirely predictable (and, indeed, that we predicted it[20]). I think there may be something of the same underlying phenomenon at work in people's desire to know the 'plan' for interest rates. In a letter to the *Financial Times* in 2018, my former colleague Martin Weale made a similar point: 'The pressure on the Bank of England for clearer communication is a consequence of people wanting the future to be less uncertain than it is.'[21]

---

[19] The oracle at Delphi foretold the future but she often spoke in riddles (encouraged, some claim, by the hallucinogenic gases emanating from fissures in nearby rocks). Presumably the name was chosen more because of the contrast with commitment: one of the inscriptions at the temple reads 'Make a pledge and mischief is nigh', sometimes shortened to 'surety brings ruin'.

[20] The first is called 'the over-confidence effect', the second 'hindsight bias'. Both are extremely well researched and documented (see, for example, Kahneman,2011). The second is ubiquitous. How often does one hear people – or, indeed, oneself – say 'X was bound to occur', or 'I always knew Y was going to happen', when neither is, in fact, true?

[21] 'The Bank of England cannot make promises about interest rates'. *Financial Times*, 4 July 2018.

Anyhow, whatever the true cause, I sometimes worry that there's a potential cost to this (one that matters more than the odd 'unreliable boyfriend' tag). If people come to rely too much on explicit steers from the central bank, forward interest rates and other asset prices may become insufficiently sensitive to economic events. And if in turn the central bank acquiesces to the desire for more definitive statements about the future path of interest rates and feels the need to signal policy changes well in advance, this could compromise its ability to respond to surprises that occur in the meantime.

The dotted line in Figure 3.6 seeks to get the point across. It's the outcome of a simulation in which the monetary authority periodically publishes a plan for future interest rates. People believe the plan, but the monetary authority only gets to change it intermittently. In the meantime, and no matter what crops up in the economy, it's obliged to follow the most recently published path. The idea is to convey the flavour of what happens when the central bank is (or feels) obliged routinely to 'pre-announce' a path for interest rates but can only update that path now and then.

Remember that this is a model in which forward interest rates have a powerful impact on current demand and economic activity. So living with the 'wrong' forward rate – one that fails to respond to incoming news – can be pretty costly. In reality the economy is almost certainly less sensitive to expected future interest rates than assumed here, and the dotted line wouldn't be so far above the others. But qualitatively, at least,

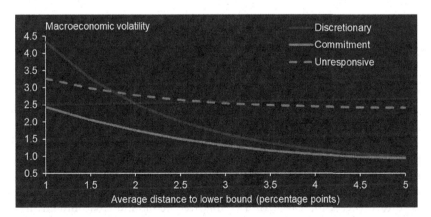

Figure 3.6 If the central bank feels obliged to 'pre-announce' a policy path in advance, this could compromise its ability to stabilise demand and inflation.

it gets the problem across. Sought for its own sake, greater stability and predictability of interest rates can come at the cost of less stability in demand and inflation (i.e. the central bank's ultimate objectives).

Conclusion

It would be nice if interest rates were more predictable. In fact, it would be nice if everything was more predictable. But many things, including stuff that might otherwise disturb inflation over the medium term, are not. And because it's the job of monetary policy to respond to such things, interest rates are also unpredictable.

There are particular circumstances in which committing more unambiguously to a future path of interest rates can be an advantage. If there's a risk of deflation, but the policy rate is stuck at the lower bound, and QE is for some reason thought to be ineffective, a declaration that policy will remain accommodative, even in the event of more inflationary pressure in the future, can in principle stimulate demand today. But even when such a commitment is believed, the effects are probably smaller than simple economic models tend to assume. Such a promise is by its nature non-credible – you know you're going to be tempted to break it – and is therefore likely to be ineffective unless there's a mechanism for keeping you to it. (Even if that were possible elsewhere, I think the hurdle to such commitments is higher in this country, given the MPC's one-person, one-vote decision-making.) This helps to explain why, in practice, central banks have made such commitments only rarely, even when the most pressing problem was the threat of low inflation. There is obviously even less of a case for it today.

Yet my impression has been that, even when central banks attempt to engage in more standard, conditional statements about future policy, they can be sometimes mistaken for firmer commitments than they really are. The potential cost is that forward interest rates, and monetary conditions more generally, become over-dependent on central bank communication and insufficiently sensitive to economic news.

Clearly the central bank has an obligation to set out its view of the economic outlook, not least to explain the stance of policy today (as distinct from what might happen to it tomorrow). That's because it takes time for policy to work and today's decision can therefore only be taken in the light of some distribution of possible economic outcomes in the future (i.e. a forecast). In a changeable economic environment, in which these things may not be so easy to infer directly, it may also want to say more about its potential reaction to such outcomes (its 'reaction function'). Expectations of future interest rates affect current demand,

and policymakers clearly have an interest in their behaving appropriately as economic news comes in.

There are various ways of doing that – speeches, simulations, perhaps even published rate paths. But whatever the medium monetary authorities need always to think that the message – not least the point that future policy will depend on how the outlook for inflation evolves – is well understood.

Technical Appendix

This appendix provides further details of the simulations reported in Figures 3.4, 3.5 and 3.6.

We use a simple New Keynesian model, in which each time period, t, is one quarter of a year:

$$x_t = \delta E_t x_{t+1} - \sigma \delta \left(i_t - E_t \pi_{t+1} - r_t^* \right)$$

$$\pi_t - \pi^* = \beta E_t \left(\pi_{t+1} - \pi^* \right) + \kappa x_t + u_t$$

where χ is the output gap, π denotes inflation and π^* denotes the inflation target. Following Haberis, Harrison and Waldron (2019), we set $\sigma = 1$ and $\kappa = 0.025$. We set $\beta = 0.995$.

Textbook New Keynesian models (e.g. Woodford, 2003; Galí, 2008) typically assume that $\delta = 1$. This in turn implies that the effect on the output gap of a change in the real interest rate in the very distant future is identical to the effect of a change in the short-term real interest rate. That property of the model gives rise to the so-called 'forward guidance puzzle' (Gabaix, 2020; Del Negro, Giannoni and Patterson, 2023). A variety of small changes to the underlying textbook model give rise to an equation for aggregate demand with $\delta < 1$ so that changes in the real interest rate in the distant future have strictly less effect on spending today than changes in real interest rates in the near term. Our implementation follows Rannenberg (2021) and we set $\delta = 0.9$, midway between the values of 0.85 and 0.96 used by Gabaix (2020) and Rannenberg (2021) respectively.

The model is driven by two exogenous shocks, which follow simple stochastic processes:

$$r_t^* - R^* = \rho_{r^*} \left(r_{t-1}^* - R^* \right) + s_{r^*} \varepsilon_t^{r^*}$$

$$u_t = s_u \varepsilon_t^u$$

We set $\rho^* = 0.85$ following Haberis, Harrison and Waldron (2019) and choose s_{r^*} and s_u so that the model implied variances of inflation, output gap and the short-term interest rate are similar to those in the data.[22] The values chosen are $s_r^* = 0.4$, $s_u = 0.15$.

The loss function used to guide monetary policy and evaluate outcomes is

$$V_t = \mathrm{E}_t \sum_{\tau=t}^{\infty} \beta^\tau \left((\pi_t - \pi^*)^2 + \lambda x_t^2 \right) = \mathrm{E}_t \sum_{\tau=t}^{\infty} \beta^\tau \mathcal{L}_t \qquad (1)$$

and $\mathcal{L}$ denotes the 'period loss' and we set $\lambda = 0.25$. This is somewhat higher than the values often implied by approximations to the utility of representative households in a textbook model (for example Woodford, 2003; Galí, 2008) but closer to the values often used by policymakers in indicative simulations (e.g. Yellen, 2012; Carney, 2017).

Our baseline assumptions for monetary policy assume that the policy-maker sets the nominal interest rate to minimise (1), subject to a lower bound on the nominal interest rate:

$$i_t \ge b$$

and the lower bound is imposed in the simulations using the algorithms described in Harrison and Waldron (2021).

The average distance of the interest rate from the lower bound is given by $R^* + \pi^* - b$. We simulate the model for alternative assumptions about the average amount of policy space and the conduct of monetary policy. In each case, the model is simulated for 256,000 periods and the average period loss, $\mathcal{L}$, is computed. The charts in the main text plot the square root of this loss, normalised to 1 for the case of commitment policy with 5% average policy space.

The model is simulated under four alternative assumptions about the conduct of monetary policy:

Discretionary policy: the policymaker sets the interest rate in a·time-consistent manner to minimise (1). Time-consistent policy means that the policymaker sets policy optimally today recognising that future policymakers will act in the same way. So today's policymaker cannot influence future policy actions and therefore cannot make credible commitments about the future path of the interest rate.

Commitment policy: the policymaker sets the interest rate according to a policy rule that minimises (1) under commitment. The commitment policy allows the policymaker to influence output and inflation in the near

---

[22] Under a simple Taylor rule for monetary policy and ignoring the zero lower bound. The resulting standard deviations for the output gap, annual inflation and the annualised policy rate are (approximately) 1.5, 1 and 2 respectively.

term by making credible promises about the behaviour of interest rates in the future.

Imperfectly credible commitment policy: the policymaker sets the interest rates according to a policy rule that minimises (1) under commitment but recognising that private agents believe that the policymaker will switch to the discretionary policy with a constant (5%) probability each period. Even though the policymaker never switches from the commitment policy, the fact that agents doubt the credibility of the policymaker's commitments implies that credible promises about the behaviour of interest rates in the future have less traction over output and inflation in the near term.

Unresponsive policy: every N period, the policymaker announces a path for the interest rate over the next K periods. The policymaker then follows the plan (for the $N - 1$ subsequent periods) and then announces a new path and the process repeats. Each announced path is consistent with the path for the interest rate under optimal commitment, conditional on *no future shocks arriving*. Because shocks subsequently *do* arrive, the policymaker is therefore unresponsive to the economic news (interest rates are set according to the pre-announced plan). For simplicity we consider the case in which $N = 2$ and $K = 4$.

References

Bailey, Andrew, Jonathan Bridges, Richard Harrison, Josh Jones and Aakash Mankodi (2020), 'The central bank balance sheet as a policy tool: Past, present and future'. Staff Working Paper No. 899.

Broadbent, Ben (2013), 'Conditional guidance as a response to supply uncertainty'. Speech given by External Member of the Monetary Policy Committee, Bank of England at the London Business School, Monday 23 September.

Broadbent (2017), 'The history and future of QE', Speech given to the Society of Professional Economists, London, 23 July 2018. www.bis.org/review/r180724c.pdf

Broadbent, Ben (2018), 'The history and future of QE'. Speech given by Deputy Governor, Monetary Policy at the Society of Professional Economists, London 23 July.

Carney, Mark (2017), 'Lambda'. Speech given by Governor of the Bank of England, London School of Economics, Monday 16 January.

Del Negro, Marco, Marc Giannone and Chrisina Patterson (2023), 'The forward guidance puzzle', *Journal of Political Economy: Macroeconomics*. 1(1), 43–79.

Feroli, Michael, David Greenlaw, Peter Hooper, Frederic Mishkin and Amir Sufi (2017), 'Language after liftoff: Fed communication away from the zero lower bound', *Research in Economics*, Elsevier. 71(3), 452–90.

Gabaix, Xavier (2020), 'A behavioral New Keynesian model', *American Economic Review*. 110(8), 2271–327.

Gali, Jordi (2008), *Monetary Policy, Inflation, and the Business Cycle*. Princeton University Press.

Haberis, Alex, Richard Harrison and Max Waldron (2019), 'Uncertain policy promises', *European Economic Review*. 111, 459–74.

Harrison, Richard and Matt Waldron (2021), 'Optimal policy with occasionally binding constraints: Piecewise linear solution methods'. Staff Working Paper No. 911 February.

Kahneman, Daniel (2011), *Thinking, Fast and Slow*. Farrar, Straus and Giroux.

King, Mervyn (2005), 'Monetary policy: Practice ahead of theory'. Speech given by Governor of the Bank of England at the Mais Lecture, Cass Business School, London 17 May.

Krugman, Paul (1999), 'It's baaack: Japan's slump and the return of the liquidity trap'. *Brookings Papers on Economic Activity*. 2, 137–87.

McDermott, John (2013), 'The role of forecasting in monetary policy'. Speech by Assistant Governor and Head of Economics of the Reserve Bank of New Zealand, to the Financial Services Institute of Australasia, Wellington, 15 March.

Miles, David (2014), 'What is the right amount of guidance? The experience of the Bank of England with forward guidance'. Speech given at the De Nederlandsche Bank annual research conference, Amsterdam, 13 November.

Norges Bank (2022), Norges Bank's Monetary Policy Handbook Issue 1 of Norges Bank papers.

Rannenberg, Ansgar (2021), 'State-dependent fiscal multipliers with preferences over safe assets', *Journal of Monetary Economics*. 117(C), 1023–40.

Riksbank (2017), The Riksbank's Experiences of Publishing Repo Rate Forecasts', Riksbank Studies, June.

Swanson, Eric and John Williams (2014), 'Measuring the effect of the zero lower bound on yields and exchange rates in the U.K. and Germany', *Journal of International Economics*. 92(Supplement 1), S2–S21.

Woodford, Michael (2003), *Interest and Prices: Foundations of a Theory of Monetary Policy*. Princeton University Press.

Woodford, Michael (2012), 'Methods of policy accommodation at the interest-rate lower bound,' in *The Changing Policy Landscape*. Proceedings of the Jackson Hole Economic Policy Symposium. Federal Reserve Bank of Kansas City, 185–288.

Yellen, Janet (2012), 'Perspectives on monetary policy', at the Boston Economic Club Dinner, Boston, Massachusetts.

4   MPC Monetary Communication
Children of the Revolution(s)

Delia Sih Chien Macaluso and Michael McMahon [1]

Introduction

Much like most of the Bank of England's regular communications, this article has both a backward-looking and a forward-looking component. Looking backward, we will document the communication successes of the Bank's Monetary Policy Committee (MPC) as it approaches its 25th anniversary, but we will also highlight where things could have been better. Turning to the future, we shall build on these last 25 years and try to suggest the ways communication needs to evolve further.

Blinder et al. (2008) define monetary policy communication broadly as 'the information that the central bank makes available about its current and future policy objectives, the current economic outlook, and the likely path for future monetary policy decisions.' As our title alludes to, there has been, since the 1980s, a monetary policy communication revolution. In fact, we will argue that there have been at least two revolutions (more if one were willing to broaden the focus to include other aspects of central bank communication). Given the focus on the MPC, we shall stick mostly to issues in monetary policy communication though we will mention other aspects of central bank communication where it is relevant.

To summarise the revolutions by broad descriptions of the questions central banks seemed to be asking themselves across different eras:[2]

- Until 1990s: 'Do we (have to) communicate this?'
- 1st Revolution ≡ 1990s to the Global Financial Crisis (GFC): 'Why wouldn't we communicate this?'
- 2nd Revolution ≡ From GFC to Now: 'How should we communicate this in a way that engages a broad cross-section of society?'

footnote[1] McMahon gratefully acknowledges financial support from the European Research Council (Consolidator Grant Agreement 819131). We thank Sean Holly, Dame Rachel Lomax, Sir John Vickers and participants at the MPC25 Conference for helpful comments. The title paraphrases, without implication, Marc Bolan of T. Rex fame. All errors and omissions are those of the authors alone.
[2] Skingsley (2019) asked similar questions.

49

The first revolution can be linked to the adoption of inflation targeting. This involved a low-frequency communication with a broad audience, the target, which was then paired with higher-frequency communication with financial market participants. This is what most monetary economists would consider the conventional communication. The second revolution followed from the decline of trust in the central bank and growing threats to central bank independence after the GFC.

In this article we discuss MPC communication accounting for differences in timing, frequencies, and target audience. These characteristics identify each tool through their design and reflect the evolution of transparent monetary policy from technically aware to increasingly democratic.

Revolution 1: Inflation Targeting, Transparency and Communication

In this section we discuss why the first revolution followed with the adoption of an inflation-targeting framework. We discuss the portfolio of communication channels and then focus on two specific issues with the Bank's communications.

Inflation Targeting and Communication

Adoption of an inflation target predates the establishment of the MPC in the UK. The first inflation target was adopted following Britain's departure from the Exchange Rate Mechanism in September 1992. Inflation-targeting regimes are based on a clear, numerical objective for inflation and a high degree of transparency and accountability. The new framework was the impetus for a lot of the first communication revolution. Even when the famous targeting inflation conference took place in 1995 at the Bank of England, while instrument control remained with the Treasury, a lot of the discussion was about the transparency and communication aspects; at the time, the Bank was quite unique (along with New Zealand) in publishing both a forecast as well as the minutes of the monetary briefing meeting (the so-called Ken and Eddie show). These publications are now standard in inflation-targeting regimes.[3]

There are two reasons for the focus on communication (sometimes called 'open mouth operations'). One is democratic accountability which clearly becomes important once the central bank gains independence.

---

[3] See Haldane (1995) or Bernanke et al. (1998) for specific discussions of the designs and implementation of IT regimes.

The other is that communication plays a central role in the management of expectations which is a central tenet of monetary policy frameworks in our theoretical models (King, Lu and Pasten, 2008). For instance, in the New Keynesian models (Gali, 2015, for example), inflation expectations are a vital determinant of inflation. The two reasons clearly overlap; to be able to influence expectations, the central bank has to be expected to act to achieve its target which requires the continued support of the government which grants it its independence. Both, therefore, are key aspects that contribute to the credibility of the central bank's monetary policy.

The MPC's Communication Portfolio

The MPC's communication involves both higher- and lower-frequency communication. Both can play a key role in inflation control by influencing how agents form their expectations.

At the lower frequency, as already suggested, there are some great communication successes. Three warrant specific discussion.

1. The inflation target itself ($\pi^\star$)

A major advantage of an inflation target is that the central bank can more easily communicate their ultimate objective. Of course, the target does not itself communicate a complete monetary reaction function, but it did eradicate the need to communicate how intermediate targets, such as money growth, are related to inflation (especially since the relationship may be volatile).

For the UK, the target was initially a range. When the Bank gained independence in 1997, the target was expressed as a point, 2.5%, based on the RPIX inflation index. But there was also a window around this target of +/−1pp. In June 2003, the Chancellor changed the index on which the target is based to the harmonised index of consumer prices (CPI) and simultaneously reduced the inflation target to 2% to account for the differences in the construction of the two indices. There was no material change in the target.

Figure 4.1 shows that, at the most basic level, the inflation-targeting regime has operated as expected. It shows that the target was never missed in the first 15 years of the inflation target (the first nine of the MPC being in charge of monetary policy).[4] Figure 4.2 shows that market-based inflation expectations, even over longer horizons, came down with inflation targeting and again with central bank independence.

---

[4] It went above target in March 2007 (3.1%), then again from May to December 2008, December 2009 to April 2012, November 2017 (3.1%), and now since August 2021. It fell below less often: December 2014 to August 2016, October 2016, April to June 2020, and August 2020 to March 2021 (Covid-19).

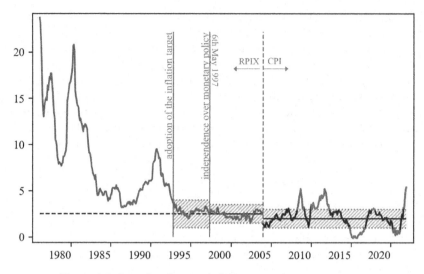

Figure 4.1 Actual and target inflation over time.
Notes: Office for National Statistics data for inflation (RPIX and then CPI) and official target information. The sample plotted is monthly frequency from 1976 to 2022.

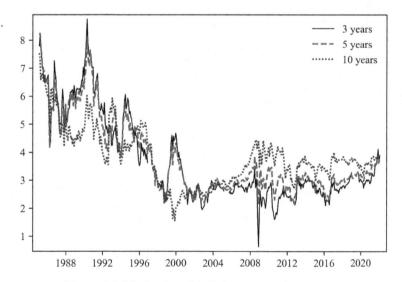

Figure 4.2 Market-based inflation expectations.
Notes: Bank of England data. The sample plotted is monthly frequency from 1985 to 2022.

2. Descriptions of the technical details of the Bank of England Monetary Policy

The Bank, in the early days of the MPC, produced many documents to describe and explain the technical and logistical details of the monetary policy process (Bean and Jenkinson, 2001), the monetary transmission mechanism (Bank of England, 1999b), the models used in the policy process (Bank of England, 1999a, 2000; Harrison et al., 2005; Burgess et al., 2013), as well as reviews of the process (Pagan, 2003, for instance) and the Bank's responses to these.[5]

These are, in general, quite wonkish and do not speak to a wide cross-section of the general public. Nonetheless, these are important documents and were vital pieces of reading for students of my generation![6]

3. Letters to the Chancellor

According to the MPC's remit, if inflation moves outside of the bands (+/−1pp) of the inflation target, the Governor must write a letter to the Chancellor of the Exchequer. In this letter, the Governor must explain why inflation has missed the target bands, how the MPC is responding, and how the committee is balancing trade-offs such as getting inflation back to target more quickly versus reducing output volatility. The Governor must write again if, after three months, inflation continues to be outside the target bands.[7]

The importance of these letters is that they ensure that the Bank must, in a relatively consistent fashion, explain a failure to achieve the target to the Chancellor and, more broadly, to politicians and the general public. This is a vital medium to allow communication on these issues and enables a vital channel of accountability for an independent MPC.

As an aside: It is not clear whether these should be seen as low frequency (we waited 13 years for the first one in May 2010); or higher frequency (we have had 23, and rising, since the first one).

At a higher frequency, the MPC, like other monetary policymakers, have several regular communication channels, and these too have been evolving. These include the Statements, Minutes, the Monetary Policy Report which was initially the Inflation Report with the Bank's forecast including the infamous fan charts and regular speeches by MPC members.

---

[5] We thank Sir John Vickers for reminding us of these important documents.

[6] These documents should be kept up to date. When searching the Bank of England website, it is found that the most recent models are not obviously described. Moreover, the transmission mechanism document has not been updated for a long time (at least publicly); in that time, the Bank has gained new policy tools such as asset purchases, macroprudential policy under the FPC which interacts with monetary policy, and it now places more emphasis on communication through forward guidance.

[7] The letter used to be sent with the release of the CPI data showing the breach. Since March 2020, the letter is published with the MPC minutes of the meeting following the breach. This allows the MPC time to understand the breach (if it was a surprise) and to deliberate and vote on policy action.

Regular appearances before the Treasury Select Committee, like the Governor's Letters to the Chancellor described above, also provide a mechanism for direct accountability which is extremely important in an era of independent monetary policy.

A major reform of the information provision took place in 2015: following the Warsh review (Warsh, 2014), the MPC began to publish all of their key releases: the decision, the minutes (including the voting record), and the Monetary Policy Report on the same day that they make the monetary policy decision, which is typically a Thursday.[8] This followed the recommendation to 'publish policy decision and rationale as soon as is practicable'. Additionally, the number of policy meetings was reduced from twelve to eight.

Prior to this, the MPC would make a statement announcing their policy decision though the post-meeting statement was typically limited (unlike the FOMC and ECB GC statements). It would contain a few paragraphs of supporting information when a change in interest rates was made but otherwise would simply read, as on 5 October 2000, 'The Bank of England's Monetary Policy Committee today voted to maintain the Bank's repo rate at 6.0%.' It would also alert the reader to the date of the minutes' release. Over time, the statement would be used more and more to reveal the economic thinking behind the decision, though the full discussion of views and votes was only released with the minutes.

Then, two weeks later, the minutes would be released containing an account of the policy decision, the members who voted for and against the proposition, and a summary of the economy in terms of the data discussed at the meeting. The importance of the minutes for the UK largely reflected its role as the key vehicle to explain the thinking of the committee and, through the votes, the dispersion of views held by members.

The lack of detail in the statement meant that forward guidance in the broad sense, which existed for the FOMC via balance of risks discussions in the statements, had to wait until the release of the minutes. The MPC minutes, and especially the release of the voting outcome, played this role signalling the likely direction of future policy (Gerlach-Kristen, 2003). The move to Super Thursday has clearly meant that such forward guidance can now accompany the immediate decision, though perhaps a move to more detailed statements could have also achieved this outcome.

For the last 25 years, the MPC has presented its forecast in the Inflation Report/Monetary Policy Report four times per year – in February, May,

---

[8] The MPC also agreed to release meeting transcripts following an eight-year lag. This applies to the March 2015 policy meeting, and so we must wait until 2023 to receive the first set of these. See Hansen, McMahon and Prat (2018) for a discussion of the impact of transcripts on FOMC deliberation.

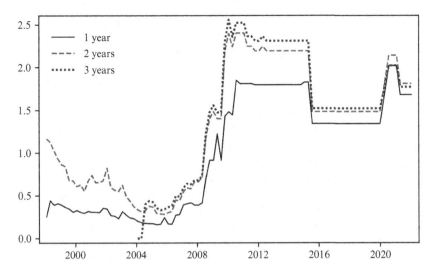

Figure 4.3 Variance of inflation projections at a one-year, two-year, and three-year horizon.
Notes: Bank of England data.

August and November. This was, in the old system, released typically six days after the MPC meeting (and a week and a day before the minutes would be released). A key communication device for the forecast is the famous fan chart figures. Introduced by the Bank in the 1996 February Inflation Report (Britton, Fisher and Whitley, 1998),[9] these forecast probability distributions have become a key tool in both the assessment and communication of forecast uncertainty. Central banks in many countries now use similar figures even though the specific construction of the distribution varies (Razi and Loke, 2017). Studies, particularly for the UK, have shown that the fan chart distribution plays a role in communicating uncertainty to market expectations; see Hansen, McMahon and Tong (2019) and Rholes and Sekhposyan (2021).

However, there is an issue about the extent to which the MPC continues to use fan charts to communicate changes in uncertainty. Figure 4.3 shows the variance parameter underlying the inflation forecast at one-, two- and three-year horizons; we use this as a measure of the uncertainty perceived by the MPC in its forecast. At all horizons, there was a large increase in uncertainty at the GFC followed by long periods of

---

[9] Initially the Bank produced the fan chart for inflation only but introduced the GDP growth fan chart in the November 1997 IR.

unchanged uncertainty.[10] Figure 4.4 shows that skewed forecasts seem to be much less prevalent than previously. Rholes and Petersen (2020) show that communicating a density around a forecast affects how effective the point forecast is at managing expectations, but also how subsequent inflation misses are treated. It is not certain that the introduction of more skewed forecasts would have better signalled the probability and direction of likely interest rate moves because even if the skew signalled the direction of concerns, the interest rate move would also depend on how the MPC chose to react to these concerns. Nonetheless, it is not clear how the MPC converged on using the fan charts in the way that they have and whether their use as a communication tool has changed.

The other mechanisms for communication of the MPC's views are speeches. These are an important aspect of the one-person-one-vote philosophy of the MPC. While some people complain about the cacophony of voices, cacophony is an important channel to communicate

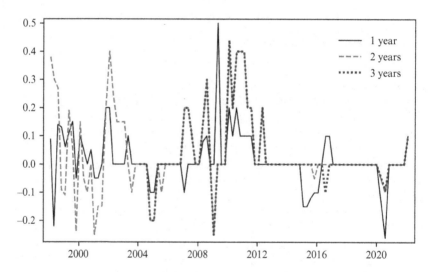

Figure 4.4 Skewness of inflation projections at a one-year, two-year, and three-year horizon.
Notes: Bank of England data.

[10] A similar pattern exists for GDP growth forecasts. These are harder to show consistently because the Bank reported the level, rather than the growth rate, of GDP between August 2020 and August 2021 (given that post-Covid-19 growth rates were very large). During this period, the standard deviation and skew were reported in billions. As such, it is not possible to easily compare the evolution of GDP uncertainty in that period.

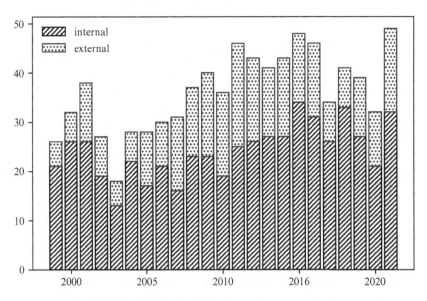

Figure 4.5 Volume of speeches and breakdown by speakers' affiliation. Notes: Bank of England data including any speeches given by members of the MPC at the time the speech was given. Early speech data from the Bank website is incomplete so the sample only begins in 1999; we stop the sample at the end of 2021.

a diversity of views and, potentially, uncertainty. Figure 4.5 shows that, over the last 25 years, MPC members on average deliver more speeches. Moreover, the breadth of information covered, topics beyond monetary policy, has also increased, especially by the internal members who have multiple committee commitments.

Two other publications deserve mention. First, the *Quarterly Bulletin*, released (as the name suggests) quarterly, is not specifically from the MPC, but it regularly presents discussions of monetary policy topics including monetary policy operations. Second, MPC members and the Bank's staff produce numerous research working papers. These, often more academic pieces, help to communicate the latest thinking about monetary economics topics and how the Bank is treating them in their analysis. The Bank has improved in the last 25 years in terms of its willingness to release research and disseminate the findings; in the past there was often a long lag in the publication process even for working papers as the Bank seemed to be worried about the research being perceived as official views (despite the 'usual disclaimer'). This trend should continue.

Specific Issue 1: How Unreliable Is the Bank as a Boyfriend?

One specific concern that has been raised about the Bank's communication is the extent to which the Bank's monetary policy actions disappointed market expectations that were heavily influenced by earlier central bank communication.[11] Specifically, the idea is that, in the months prior to a meeting, MPC members may hint at a particular move such that this action is priced in by investors; when these hints fail to translate into action at the subsequent meeting, it generates a market surprise (and some annoyance from investors). In these cases, the Bank has been likened to an 'unreliable boyfriend'.[12]

The most recent was after the MPC meeting of November 2021. In late September, the Governor was seen to strike a more hawkish tone in a speech at the Society of Professional Economists' annual dinner. In October, the Governor had expressed greater urgency for the Bank, and other central banks, to act on rising inflation. The markets took a clear message of the Bank's intention to hike rates before the end of the year. If we look at Figure 4.6a reporting the time series for the estimated number of 0.25% movements priced into overnight index swaps for the November 4 meeting, we can see that the underlying expectation was of no rate change until Bailey's speech (September 27), when the market started to price in the probability of a hike and then moved further towards certainty of a change after the G30 declaration (October 17). Markets also expected future policy rate increases in the December and February meetings.

The MPC left interest rates unchanged in November, taking financial markets by surprise. On the day of the meeting, markets had to face the sudden realisation that the expected tightening would not be forthcoming as can be inferred from the abrupt adjustments in the series for the December and February meetings. When confronted with accusation that he had, like his predecessor, displayed unreliable tendencies, he clarified that his statement was a conditional one upon the transient, or not, nature of inflation and the lingering repercussions of the pandemic.

---

[11] Of course, the way in which central banks communicate and the extent to which they conduct forward guidance go beyond the Bank of England. In providing forward guidance, it is itself a communication issue to ensure that markets understand the nature of that guidance. In particular, to what extent the guidance is Odyssean, giving a commitment to a future path, or Delphic which is state-dependent guidance.

[12] The moniker was first used by MP Pat McFadden in 2014 in relation to the then Governor Mark Carney; the MPC chose to forego the forward guidance policy for more ambiguous statements. It has been picked up several times since then, whenever the Bank didn't act consistently with the expectations previously set by themselves.

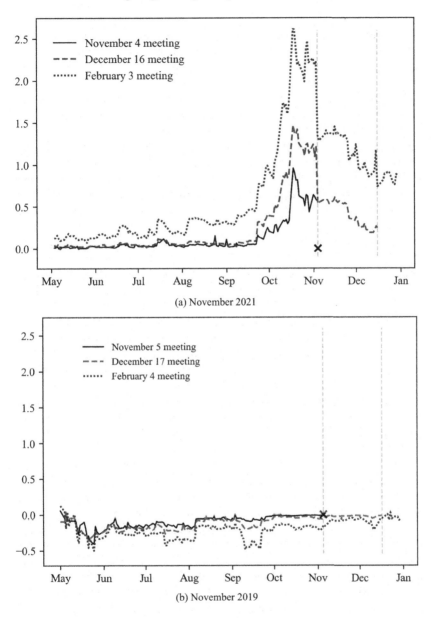

(a) November 2021

(b) November 2019

Figure 4.6 Market expectations on future actions.
Notes: Bloomberg data. The daily estimated number of 0.25% movements forecasted for each meeting as priced into the contemporaneous overnight index swaps forward curve for the UK at market close.

For comparison, Figure 4.6b reports the priced-in movements for a meeting two years before: while there is still some underlying variation over time imputable to market movements, this is of a completely different magnitude and, more importantly, eventually does not lead to surprise on the day of the meeting.

Clearly markets are very attentive to developing sentiments across the MPC that might hint at what the following action might be. One typical way to communicate different views is through speeches which typically include commentary on the state of the economy and sometimes propose appropriate actions when the economy might veer away from achieving the inflation target. The focus on these speeches means that members need to be very careful about what they want to communicate and the way to communicate it to markets effectively – in particular, communicating any conditionality.

The more formal way that MPC members express disagreement is through their voting behaviour in meetings. The MPC has typically enjoyed a reputation for sincere and democratic voting, the one-person-one-vote philosophy becoming particularly clear in August 2005 when the Governor voted on the losing side of a decision to cut rates.

More recently, the question arose as to whether the committee was dissenting less. Had there been a shift towards debating disagreements behind closed doors and presenting a united front to the public? This wouldn't be a novelty in itself; it has been a common practice for the FOMC. Figures 4.7 and 4.8 show voting dissent patterns over the years. Even accounting for the zero lower bound (ZLB) period[13] where a more inertial behaviour can be reconciled with a floor for the policy rate, the data for policy rate and asset purchases seems to be consistent with less dissent than initially.

While we can quantitatively measure the extent of the dissent in voting, there can be many underlying reasons for voting differences: different opinions on the current state of the economy, alternative views of how it will evolve, and disagreement on the optimal policy action.

And, of course, MPC members can disagree to agree. That is, because the economy is complex and dynamic, differences in beliefs about the current state of the economy, as emphasised in Byrne et al. (2023), can coexist with different beliefs about the likely dynamics of the economy, such that MPC members agree on the future outlook and the appropriate policy choice.[14] Similarly, the committee might have different views on

---

[13] We refer to ZLB period as the time frame for which the range of policy rates was entirely below 0.5%.

[14] There is uncertainty about the horizon at which monetary policy has its maximum effect on the economy (estimates vary anywhere from 18 months to three years), and the effect

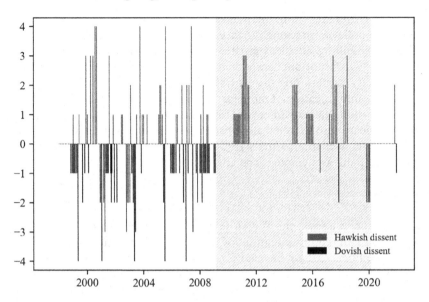

Figure 4.7 Voting discrepancy on interest rate changes over time.
Notes: Number of votes in favour of a higher or lower (grey and black) rate compared to the majority.

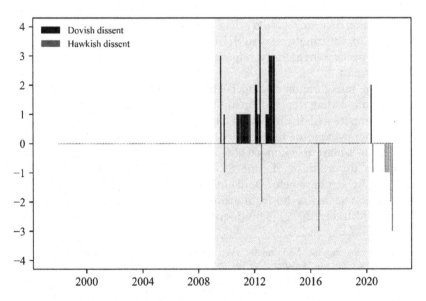

Figure 4.8 Voting discrepancy on asset purchases over time.
Notes: Number of votes in favour of a higher or lower (grey and black) asset purchase volume compared to majority.

what the correct reaction function should be, such that they agree on the choice of policy even though their views on the economic outlook differ. These possibilities are likely greater at the ZLB, where the already noisy signal loses an important component, the economy being constrained and the liquidity trap limiting the central bank's ability to stimulate it.

Also, communication of monetary policy becomes more difficult when there are multiple instruments. This means that it is possibly harder to communicate with as much clarity as in the past since the GFC when the instruments available to the MPC have expanded (and even more so when the Bank as a whole is considered).

Specific Issue 2: Super Thursday and Information Overload

As mentioned above, the Warsh review brought significant changes to the timing of communication of MPC decisions and analysis. On 11 December 2014, the MPC introduced 'Super Thursday' on which their decision, the minutes (including the voting record) and the Monetary Policy Report (in the relevant months) are now published on the same day. The logic was to enhance the effectiveness of its communications, and its accountability, and to address the lack of a detailed policy statement. (To accommodate these communication changes, the MPC also adjusted the logistics around the meeting.)

Eichengreen and Geraats (2015) worried that the changes would worsen transparency rather than strengthen it. In particular, the 'deluge' of information would make the logistical changes to the meeting process negatively impact the ability to make the best possible decision.

Did the introduction of Super Thursday lead to noticeable errors of interpretation that were not made in the earlier period? How do such errors compare with the impact of having markets have to wait (and trade) without knowledge of the detailed reasons for a policy decision? It is difficult to isolate the impact of Super Thursday. One simple exercise compares the amount of time for the OIS market price to settle on Inflation Report days before and after Super Thursday; the time to digest information seems to go from around 35 mins to around 60 mins on average (Munday, 2022). This doesn't seem too concerning. But enough

---

is likely time-varying. Additionally, even though the Bank has an inflation target, its secondary objective is 'subject to [price stability], [it] support[s] the Government's economic policy, including its objectives on growth and employment'. Therefore, within reasonable bounds, it is a matter of individual decision how to evaluate the trade-off between the nominal and real sides of the economy and assess the costs of, say, a temporary rise in inflation to alleviate unemployment pressures.

time has passed that it would be good for the Bank to do a review of these changes and, if necessary, fine-tune the communication of monetary policy. This may be especially useful since the communication of policy has, since 2017, been broadened to include a wider cross-section of society. We now turn to this issue in more detail.

Revolution 2: Broader Communication

Haldane (2017) emphasised the emergence of both a deficit of public understanding about the central bank and a deficit of public trust in central banks. These developments potentially make the Bank's monetary policy less effective and undermine their ability to achieve the inflation target and weaken the impact of their communications. The second revolution concerns the attempts by the Bank to rebuild trust in the institution following the GFC. Other central banks are making similar attempts – see Blinder et al. (2022) for a broad discussion of the literature on communication with the general public.

Haldane and McMahon (2018) consider four reasons to address the general public:

1. Households are central to economic activity: their expectations matter and so communication can help the central bank to control or influence the narrative (Shiller, 2017).
2. Building public understanding may be important as a means of establishing trust and credibility about central banks and their policies. This is important not only for shaping expectations but also for reasons of political accountability,[15] ensuring operationally independent central banks are meeting the terms of their social contract with wider society.
3. The availability of clearer, more straightforward messaging might even benefit the more technical, traditional audiences. They can always get into the details later.
4. To the extent that MPCs aggregate information (Hansen, McMahon and Velasco, 2014), perhaps wider engagement also improves information sets by starting a two-way dialogue with a broader set of economic agents.

With the November 2017 Inflation Report release, the Bank of England began to release simplified ('layered') content describing the main messages; many central banks have now followed their lead. The emerging message from the research on such simplified communication is that, in

---

[15] There is an empirical correlation such that those with greater understanding and satisfaction in the Bank have better anchored inflation expectations even controlling for all the demographic controls that stratified the responses (Haldane and McMahon, 2018).

information provision experiments, it can go a long way to achieving the aims of expectation management and trust building (Haldane and McMahon, 2018; Coibion et al., 2021; Haldane, Macaulay and McMahon, 2021). However, there has been less evidence from the general population that the implemented measures have meaningfully impacted expectations.[16]

McMahon and Naylor (2023) examine whether what matters in terms of explanation is simplicity of language or simplicity of concept. Simple language, or semantic simplicity, relates to how difficult it is to read the text; it is often measured by Flesch-Kinkaid reading age scores which indicate how many years of education are needed to read a particular text. Conceptual simplicity relates to how well the reader understands the topics being discussed; it can be measured by counting the occurrence of different technical concepts such as GDP. McMahon and Naylor (2023) find that the latter matters most.

This is important because the initial layered content reduced complexity along both dimensions. But, since the introduction of layered communication, conceptual complexity has increased a lot while semantic complexity has remained low. This suggests that one reason we might not see big effects from the layered content is that it simply hasn't been targeted correctly.

Two further issues emerge. First, Haldane, Macaulay and McMahon (2021) emphasise the need to not just explain but also engage and educate. On engagement, clearly explained communication will count for nothing if people don't engage with these communications. Do they read what the central bank writes? Do they follow the Twitter account? Do they actively seek layered communication of the Bank's analysis? In the research, participants are typically incentivised to engage, and the prior engagement is not great. Thirty-four per cent had never heard of the Inflation Report while only six per cent claim to have ever read it – in fact, the reverse combination.

Engagement without understanding might not be as bad if the engagement contributes to building and maintaining trust. Joseph, Lam and McMahon (2021) look at the impact of Citizens' Panels which are another initiative launched by the Bank that aims to engage (not just explain). The emerging evidence on such two-way communication is encouraging, albeit these can only reach relatively small numbers of people.

On education, there is a worry that people read the messages, but they quickly become confused by the complexity of the economy. For

---

[16] There is anecdotal evidence that people appreciate the layered content.

instance, the concepts of 'inflation' and 'GDP' (central to policy discussions) are not well understood by the general public (Runge and Hudson-Sharp, 2020). Moreover, better economic education appears to be positively correlated with trust and likely reduces the costs of engagement. Of course, there is an important question about who should be responsible for economics education. Overall, this second revolution is still in its infancy and, we believe, is important.

In that sense, there is still a lot to learn. We are a long way from getting it right. As Blinder (2018) predicted: 'Central banks will keep trying to communicate with the general public, as they should. But for the most part, they will fail.'

Is a 3rd Revolution Coming?

Before concluding, it is worth looking ahead to think about what the next revolution might be. There are two broad, ongoing issues for the MPC, and the Bank of England more generally, in terms of communication that may be considered potential drivers of major change in communication strategy. These are (i) communication and alternative monetary frameworks and (ii) the link between monetary communication and communication on other objectives or even other issues. We briefly discuss each in turn.

Discussions about the exact details of the monetary framework, or the desirability of a different framework, continue (as they should). There is a large body of work examining the theoretical properties of different monetary regimes (Clarida, Gali and Gertler (1999) is a classic reference but there are many others). However, this literature largely takes as given the precise communication of the central bank's policies and objectives and the incorporation of these policies into expectations. We know that this is not always so. We believe, therefore, that it is important that the communication dimensions of any alternative frameworks are assessed more carefully than is typically done in theoretical assessments. For example, while there are some desirable characteristics of price-level targeting, communication of it is not as straight forward, and adopting the policy may weaken, rather than strengthen, the central bank's nominal anchor and its control of real interest rates.

This also applies to changes within the existing inflation target regime. For instance, raising the inflation target may be desirable in the sense that it reduces the probability of being constrained by the effective lower bound on nominal interest rates. But switching could involve large costs if it reduces credibility or trust in the target. To be effective, there needs to be careful consideration of the timing of such changes, and these need to be communicated in a way that shifts and then anchors expectations at the new target (Reichlin et al., 2021).

This would necessitate a three-pronged strategy. First, it is important that monetary policy acts in a manner that achieves the new inflation target. This is hard because of the stochastic nature of actual outcomes meaning that some luck might be needed to build the credibility of the new regime. Second, the change must be communicated effectively to financial markets. While this audience is engaged and can understand the reasons for the change, it must not come across as the central bank trying to shift the goal posts when they have been missing their target for a long period. Third, communication with the general public will be more difficult given they are less engaged. Coibion et al. (2021) show that the Fed's shift to average inflation targeting has had very little impact on household expectations.

The second issue concerns communication about other objectives and other issues. Since the GFC, the Bank has a broader set of policies and responsibilities. Four of the five internal MPC members additionally sit on the Financial Policy Committee (FPC) and the Prudential Regulation Committee. This has advantages because knowledge of the health of the financial system can clearly be important for the conduct of monetary policy. But the risk is that given the complex nature of the interaction between macroprudential policies, financial stability and monetary policy, speeches on financial topics might be difficult to interpret in terms of what they mean for monetary policy.

With respect to other issues, this also poses a potential difficulty. Climate change itself, as well as policies to address the risks posed by it such as carbon taxes, is a source of shocks which monetary policy must react to. Climate risks have implications for monetary operations. While climate change naturally has an impact on the economy and the financial system, the extent to which central banks actively engage in the discussion on climate policy remains controversial.[17]

In terms of monetary communication, the MPC needs to be careful to communicate how these issues feed into the monetary policy discussions. On the one hand, discussion of pertinent issues can increase engagement with the central bank and increase their perceived relevance among the public. On the other hand, as with other policy discussions, there is a risk that speaking about other issues will complicate or dilute the communication of key messages on monetary policy.

---

[17] The ECB's strategy review presented a plan to incorporate climate considerations into monetary policy as discussed in Reichlin et al. (2021).

Conclusion

The Bank of England and MPC have been at the forefront of monetary communications. This is true of both conventional communication with financial markets and, more recently, communication with the wider public. But there are still areas for improvement.

While a widespread engagement is to be encouraged, communication difficulties can arise when there is a multiplicity of forms of communication and a multiplicity of policies: ultimately the key is to make sure that the right message reaches each group, avoiding noise and confusion, and being aware of the fact that each plays a different role in the economy.

The clarity of communication, and especially of any conditionality of statements, can help avoid accusations of being an unreliable boyfriend. And the Bank should be seen to be regularly reviewing how it operates.

When evaluating the mandate or operation of monetary policy, it is key that the communication aspects are carefully considered. This is true of both future developments in terms of regime shifts and secondary objectives, as any ulterior motive carries the risk of diluting the message killing the main advantage of an inflation-targeting framework.

Communication will continue to evolve. This may be a new approach to communication, or the evolution may involve a reversion back to previous approaches. In either case, remember that just as communication has developed to enhance transparency, so too must transparency concerns guide the development of communication. As T. Rex taught us: 'No you won't fool the children of the revolution'. What they didn't mention was that you might lose your hard-earned credibility trying.

References

Bank of England (1999a), *Economic Models at the Bank of England.*

Bank of England (1999b), 'The transmission mechanism of monetary policy'. *Bank of England Quarterly Bulletin*, May.

Bank of England (2000), *Economic Models at the Bank of England: September 2000 Update.*

Bean, Charles and Nigel Jenkinson (2001), 'The formulation of monetary policy at the Bank of England'. Bank of England Quarterly Bulletin, Winter.

Bernanke, Ben, Thomas Laubach, Frederic Mishkin and Adam Posen (1998), *Inflation Targeting: Lessons from the International Experience.* Princeton University Press.

Blinder, Alan S. (2018), 'Through a crystal ball darkly: The future of monetary policy communication', *AEA Papers and Proceedings.* 108, 567–71.

Blinder, Alan S., Michael Ehrmann, Marcel Fratzscher, Jakob De Haan and David-Jan Jansen (2008), 'Central bank communication and monetary policy: A survey of theory and evidence', *Journal of Economic Literature*. 46(4), 910–45.

Blinder, Alan S, Michael Ehrmann, Jakob De Haan, and David-Jan Jansen (2022), 'Central bank communication with the general public: Promise or false hope?' CEPR Discussion Papers DP17441, Centre for Economic Policy Research.

Britton, Erik, Paul Fisher and John Whitley (1998), 'The inflation report projections: Understanding the fan chart. Bank of England Quarterly Bulletin, Q1.

Burgess, Stephen, Emilio Fernandez-Corugedo, Charlotta Groth et al. (2013), 'The Bank of England's forecasting platform: Compass, maps, ease and the suite of models'. Bank of England Working Paper, No 471.

Byrne, David, Robert Goodhead, Michael McMahon and Conor Parle (2023), 'The central bank crystal ball: Temporal information in monetary policy communication'. CEPR Discussion Paper 17930.

Clarida, Richard, Jordi Gali and Mark Gertler (1999), 'The science of monetary policy: A new Keynesian perspective', *Journal of Economic Literature*. 37(4), 1661–707.

Coibion, Olivier, Yuriy Gorodnichenko, Edward S. Knotek II and Raphael Schoenle (2021), 'Average inflation targeting and household expectations'. NBER Working Papers 27836, National Bureau of Economic Research.

Eichengreen, Barry and Petra Geraats (2015), 'The Bank of England fails its transparency test'. VoxEU, 06 January.

Gali, Jordi (2015), *Monetary Policy, Inflation, and the Business Cycle: An Introduction to the New Keynesian Framework and Its Applications*. Princeton University Press.

Gerlach-Kristen, Petra (2003), 'Insiders and outsiders at the Bank of England'. *Central Banking*, XIV(1), 96–102.

Haldane, Andrew ed. (1995), *Targeting Inflation: A Conference of Central Banks on the Use of Inflation Targets Organised by the Bank of England*. Bank of England.

Haldane, Andrew (2017), 'A little more conversation, a little less action'. A speech given at the Federal Reserve Bank of San Francisco, Macroeconomics and Monetary Policy Conference, 31 March.

Haldane, Andrew and Michael McMahon (2018), 'Central bank communications and the general public', *AEA Papers and Proceedings, American Economic Association*. 108, 578–83.

Haldane, Andrew, Alistair Macaulay and Michael McMahon (2021), 'The 3 Es of central bank communication with the public', in Ernesto Pastén and Ricardo Reis (eds.), *Independence, Credibility, and Communication of Central Banking*, 279–342. Banco Central de Chile, Santiago, Chile.

Hansen, Stephen, Michael McMahon and Carlos Velasco (2014). 'Preferences or private assessments on a monetary policy committee?', *Journal of Monetary Economics*. 67, 16–32.

Hansen, Stephen, Michael McMahon and Andrea Prat (2018), 'Transparency and deliberation within the FOMC: A computational linguistics approach'. *The Quarterly Journal of Economics*. 1332(1), 801–70.

Hansen, Stephen, Michael McMahon and Matthew Tong (2019), 'The long-run information effect of central bank communication', *Journal of Monetary Economics*. 108(C), 185–202.

Harrison, Richard, Meghan Quinn, Gareth Ramsay and Alisdair Scott (2005), *The Bank of England's Quarterly Model*. Bank of England.

Joseph, Andreas, Jenny Lam and Michael McMahon (2021), 'The public economist: Learning from our citizens' panels about the UK economy', *Bank of England Quarterly Bulletin*. 61(4). www.bankofengland.co.uk/quarterly-bul letin/2021/2021-q4/the-public-economist-learning-from-our-citizens-panels-a bout-the-uk-economy.

King, Robert G., Yang K. Lu and Ernesto S. Pastén (2008), 'Managing expectations', *Journal of Money, Credit and Banking*. 40(8), 1625–66.

McMahon, Michael and Matthew Naylor (2023), 'Getting through: Communicating complex central bank messages'. CEPR Discussion Paper.

Munday, Tim (2022), 'More than words: Bank of England publications and market prices'. BankUnderground, 17 May 2022. https://bankunderground .co.uk/2022/05/17/more-than-words-bank-of-england-publications-and-mar ket-prices/.

Pagan, Adrian (2003), 'Report on modelling and forecasting at the Bank of England'. Bank of England Quarterly Bulletin, Q1.

Razi, Ahmad and Po Ling Loke (2017), 'Fan chart: The art and science of communicating uncertainty', in Bank for International Settlements, (ed.), *IFC Bulletins Chapters in: Statistical Implications of the New Financial Landscape*, volume 43. Bank for International Settlements.

Reichlin, Lucrezia, Klaus Adam, Warwick J. McKibbin et al. (2021), *The ECB Strategy: The 2021 Review and Its Future*, volume Centre for Economic Policy Research eBook. Centre for Economic Policy Research. September.

Rholes, Ryan and Luba Petersen (2020), 'Should central banks communicate uncertainty in their projections?' Discussion papers dp20-01, Simon Fraser University, Department of Economics.

Rholes, Ryan and Tatevik Sekhposyan (2021), 'Central bank density forecasts and asset prices: Do revisions to higher-order moments matter?' mimeo.

Runge, Johnny and Nathan Hudson-Sharp (2020), 'Public understanding of economics and economic statistics'. ESCoE Occasional Papers ESCOE-OP -03, Economic Statistics Centre of Excellence.

Shiller, Robert J (2017) 'Narrative Economics', *American Economic Review*. 107(4), 967–1004.

Skingsley, Cecilia (2019), 'How to open up a central bank and why stay open?' Keynote lecture at the Central bank communications conference 'From Mystery to Transparency' organised by the Central Banks of Ukraine and Poland. Kiev, 23 May.

Warsh, Kevin (2014), Transparency and the Bank of England's Monetary Policy Committee, Review. December.

5   Central Bank Communication
Never Excuse, Never Explain

Stephen Millard

Introduction

For most of the 20th century and earlier, central banks went about their business without ever feeling the need to communicate what they were doing to the financial markets or the general public. Then from around 1990 onwards, central banks became ever more transparent, trying to make clear to the markets and the public what they were doing and why. The purpose of this review chapter is to understand why this change came about and how successful it has been. I start with a brief history of central banks and their (lack of) communication with the public. I then move on to discuss what information central banks need to transmit to financial market participants and the general public and why they might want to do this. I then discuss 'forward guidance' as a potential policy tool before evaluating the success (or otherwise) of the increase in central bank communication. I finish by concluding that clear central bank communication is important for both democratic accountability and monetary policy effectiveness.

A Brief History of Central Bank Communication

The Bank of England was founded in 1694 as a private bank whose main purpose was to fund the government when at war. Over time, the Bank developed into the United Kingdom's central bank, acting as the banker for the banks and thus forming the centre of the payment system. This was formalised in the Bank Charter Act of 1844, which granted the Bank of England a monopoly on note issue. Similarly, the Federal Reserve Act of 1913 established the Federal Reserve System 'to furnish an elastic currency, to afford means of rediscounting commercial paper, to establish a more effective supervision of banking in the US, and for other purposes'.

After World War I, both the Bank of England, under Montagu Norman, and the Federal Reserve, led by Ben Strong, the Governor of the New York Fed, increasingly pursued active monetary policies, seeking to stabilise prices while supporting the economy. But neither felt any need to communicate what they were doing with the general public. Montagu Norman, in particular, worked according to the maxim 'Never excuse, never explain'. He, and other central bankers of his time, regarded central banking as something that the general public could not understand and that would only be negatively affected if they tried to intervene or comment on it.

And this view of central banking held until relatively recently. Alan Greenspan (2007), for example, noted that at the Federal Reserve 'you soon learn to mumble with great incoherence'. Goodfriend (1986) describes the Federal Reserve's arguments at the time for pursuing monetary policy in secret. They argued that disclosure would lead to unfair speculation, since only large speculators were able to use the information to their benefit, the wrong reaction from the market, the possibility that the market might react in a way that would raise the cost of issuing debt for the government, the possibility that agents in the economy would think the FOMC had pre-committed to a particular path for rates and problems smoothing interest rates.

The first modern move towards transparency in the central banking community came in 1989 with the Reserve Bank of New Zealand Act. This instituted an 'Inflation Targeting' regime, where the Reserve Bank had a clear role, namely to operate an independent monetary policy so as to keep inflation within a target band set by the government. And, in particular, the Governor was obliged to start communicating with the markets and the general public. The main argument for imposing this was one of democratic accountability; in other words, voters had a right to know what their central bank was up to and why. But it could also be argued that monetary policy itself was more effective if financial market participants understood what central banks were up to and why as then financial markets would move in a predictable way for central banks.

Canada and the UK soon followed with inflation targets and communication was also a key part of the regime in these cases. In particular, the Bank of England started publishing its Inflation Report in 1993 and was given the ability to set monetary policy independently in 1997. The Federal Reserve, however, was much slower in adopting this framework. It was only in 1994 that the Federal Reserve started announcing its target Federal Funds interest rate and make press statements, and it was only in 2012 that they officially announced an inflation target of 2% (though it was widely understood that they had been targeting inflation at 2% prior to that date). Interestingly, the ECB provided press conferences right from the start of its Governing Council meetings in June 1998.

When the Bank of England was first charged with producing an Inflation Report the goal was 'to provide a regular report on the progress being made towards the Government's inflation objective'. The first Inflation Report came out in February 1993 and contained four sections: recent price developments, recent cost developments, the outlook for inflation and a conclusion. In other words, 'where we are now' and 'where might we be going'. What was missing was 'what this means for policy', perhaps unsurprising given that the government (specifically, the Chancellor of the Exchequer) was still setting monetary policy at that point based partly on advice from the Bank of England (what was known as 'the Ken and Eddie Show').

What Should Central Banks Communicate and Why?

In order to carry out effective monetary policy, a central bank needs to understand the degree of inflationary pressure in the economy. This implies a need to understand where the economy is now and what this means for the future evolution of the economy. Given this understanding, the central bank can adjust monetary policy in order to affect the future evolution of the economy in a way that ensures inflation is on target in the medium term. But the transmission of monetary policy through the economy will depend on the responses of households and firms and these responses, in turn, will depend on the beliefs of households and firms about where the economy is now as well as their expectations about the future path of the economy and monetary policy.

Given that, if the central bank wants its policy to have predictable effects, it needs to 'steer' the beliefs of households and firms about the current state of the economy and its future path into line with the central bank's own beliefs. And then, it needs households and firms to expect the same path for monetary policy as would be implied by the central bank's reaction function. So the central bank needs to communicate 'where we are now', 'where might we be going' and 'what this means for policy'.

From the start, the Bank of England's Inflation Report (as was then) provided an authoritative analysis of the current state of the UK economy and a forecast for where GDP growth and, most importantly, inflation were headed. But turning to 'what this means for policy' it was thought that simply providing the inflation forecast would be enough: if inflation is likely to be above target in the medium term, absent a policy intervention today, then policy needs to be tightened whereas if inflation is likely to be below target in the medium term, absent a policy intervention today, then policy needs to be loosened.

But maybe it's not as simple as that. Where the forecast is conditioned on the assumption of constant interest rates (as was the case in the Inflation Report until May 2004), the central bank has a choice between adjusting policy a little today and adjusting policy by more at a point later in the future. Adopting the latter approach creates a communication issue as it would involve showing inflation away from target in the medium term at the same time as no policy change had taken place, begging the question: why not?

When the forecast is conditioned on the market curve, a forecast of inflation away from target in the medium term suggests that the financial markets are expecting a different path for monetary policy to that expected by policymakers. This may be because the markets disagree with the policymakers' assessment of current inflationary pressure or because the markets do not understand the policymakers' reaction function. Either way, in this case there is a clear need for communication between the policymakers and the markets in order that the market curve may move in line with what is needed to ensure inflation is on target in the medium term.

But why not simply communicate the expected path of interest rates and/or quantitative easing (QE) in the first place? Some central banks such as the Norges Bank and the Sveriges Riksbank produce a forecast for the path of interest rates as part of their overall forecast. But others, including the Bank of England, have argued strongly against doing this using the Federal Reserve's argument reported in Goodfriend (1986), namely they did not want to be taken as precommitting to a particular path for interest rates lest agents should take them to task were the actual path different. Of course, this changed in 2013 with the arrival of Mark Carney as Governor and the advent of 'forward guidance' by the Bank of England.

Communicating Future Policy: Odyssean versus Delphic Communication

In the wake of the GFC, central banks worldwide cut interest rates to levels close to (or in some cases at or below) the zero lower bound. At the same time, many adopted so-called 'unconventional' monetary policy including asset purchases and – most important for our story – 'forward guidance'. In its policy statements from December 2008 onwards, the Federal Reserve made a series of statements about it expecting low interest rates to prevail 'for some time', eventually changing the language to 'at least until xx', that is, putting specific dates on the earliest time at which interest rates might increase. In August 2013, the Monetary Policy

Committee of the Bank of England committed to holding interest rates at 0.5% at least until the unemployment rate had fallen below 7%, subject to the inflation forecast remaining lower than 2.5%, inflation expectations remaining anchored, and there being no risk to financial stability.[1]

The basic idea behind forward guidance is relatively simple: commit to holding nominal interest rates at a low level into the future, which raises inflation expectations and so lowers real interest rates today. That way, central banks can loosen monetary policy despite nominal interest rates being at their lower bound.[2] But, as noted by Campbell et al. (2012), such a policy prescription may not be 'time consistent' in that once the central bank arrives at the point where it had committed to holding interest rates low, it has no incentive to follow through with the commitment. Rather it will set interest rates at that point based on economic conditions at that time. Campbell et al. referred to this type of forward guidance as 'Odyssean' because it involved the central bank tying its hands in the same way that Odysseus was tied to the mast of his ship by his crew so that he would not be drawn to his death by the sirens' song. The difference is that he could not untie himself whereas central banks clearly can.

But is this how central banks have actually used forward guidance? An alternative approach sees announcements about future policy as providing information to the markets (and the general public) about the central bank's policy reaction function, that is, how it would respond if the economy evolved in a particular way. This could be particularly useful if the central banks wanted to convey a change in its policy reaction function, for example, that it would pursue 'looser' policy than might have been expected given its past policy movements. Campbell et al. (2012) refer to this as 'Delphic' forward guidance after the famous oracle at Delphi. Specifically, they state that 'Delphic forward guidance publicly states a forecast of macroeconomic performance and likely or intended monetary policy actions based on the policymaker's potentially superior information about future macroeconomic fundamentals and its own policy goals'. This is, of course, nothing more than the communication of where the economy is now, where it's expected to head, and what the policy implications of this are, exactly what I discussed earlier!

Campbell et al. (2012) note that the Oracle at Delphi was famed for making prophecies that could easily be misinterpreted but state that they merely refer to central banks making statements about the future. To my

---

[1] As it was, the Bank Rate remained at 0.5% until August 2018, by which time the unemployment rate had fallen to 4.1%! As discussed later, this turned out to be a classic example of 'Delphic ambiguity'.

[2] See Krugman (1999), Eggertsson and Woodford (2003) and Werning (2011) for more sophisticated versions of this argument.

mind, however, it is worth thinking about the extent to which central bank 'Delphic' forward guidance is as clear and unambiguous as assumed by Campbell et al. Indeed, much of the recent literature on central bank communication has asked exactly that question.

Evaluation

Are central banks clear in their communication or are they 'Delphic' in the sense of being open to misinterpretation?

One way of testing this is to examine what happens in response to monetary policy decisions. On the assumption that the central bank has communicated to the markets exactly where the economy is now and where it thinks the economy is going, as well as its monetary policy reaction function, then there should be no market response to a monetary policy announcement. Rather, data surprises should provoke a market reaction reflecting its knowledge of the central bank's reaction function. Unfortunately, Lasaosa (2005) found that the increased communication and transparency of the Monetary Policy Committee (MPC) in the UK, post Bank of England independence, did not lead to a smaller response of financial markets to interest rate announcements. Indeed, Chadha and Nolan (2001) found that the volatility of market interest rates actually increased on monetary policy announcement days, and this could be seen in the market reaction to the MPC decision to leave rates unchanged in November 2021. The MPC were 'Delphic' in the sense of being open to misinterpretation.

Haberis et al. (2017) start from the position that 'Delphic' forward guidance creates uncertainty. In particular, forward guidance along the lines of 'interest rates shall remain fixed at least until unemployment falls below x%' (e.g., the MPC Forward Guidance of 2013 discussed earlier) leaves the public uncertain about whether interest rates will rise at that point or, instead, 'lift off' continues to be delayed. In addition, where the guidance is not 'time consistent' (in a way, the whole point of it), the public will remain uncertain about whether it will be followed through. Again, the argument is precisely that forward guidance is 'Delphic' because it is open to misinterpretation.

Conclusion

I have discussed how and why central banks started communicating their actions with the financial markets and the general public. I have argued that not only does democratic accountability demand that independent central banks explain their actions but that monetary policy itself will be more effective if financial market participants understood what central banks are up to and why. More specifically, if the central bank wants its policy to have predictable effects, it needs to bring the beliefs of agents in the economy about 'where we are now', 'where might we be going' and 'what this means for policy' close to the central bank's own beliefs. That is, it needs to communicate in a way defined by Campbell et al. (2012) as 'Delphic'. Unfortunately, central banks – like the oracle at Delphi – are still often misunderstood, with sometimes negative (economic) effects resulting.

References

Campbell, Jeffrey R, Evans, Charles L, Fisher, Jonas D M and Justiniano, Alessandro (2012), 'Macroeconomic effects of Federal Reserve forward guidance', *Brookings Papers on Economic Activity*. 43, 1–80.

Chadha, Jagjit S and Nolan, Charles (2001), 'Inflation targeting, transparency and interest rate volatility: Ditching 'monetary mystique' in the United Kingdom', *Journal of Macroeconomics*. 23, 349–66.

Eggertsson, Gauti B and Woodford, Michael (2003), 'The zero bound on interest rates and optimal monetary policy', *Brookings Papers on Economic Activity*. 34, 139–235.

Goodfriend, Marvin (1986), 'Monetary mystique: Secrecy and central banking', *Journal of Monetary Economics*. 17, 63–92.

Greenspan, Alan (2007), *The Age of Turbulence*. Penguin Press.

Haberis, Alex, Harrison, Richard and Waldron, Matthew (2017), 'Uncertain forward guidance', Bank of England Working Paper No. 654.

Krugman, Paul R (1998), 'It's baaack: Japan's slump and the return of the liquidity trap', *Brookings Papers on Economic Activity*, 29, 137–206.

Lasaosa, Ana (2005), 'Learning the rules of the new game? Comparing the reactions in financial markets to announcements before and after the Bank of England's operational independence', Bank of England Working Paper No. 255.

Werning, Ivan (2011), 'Managing a liquidity trap: Monetary and fiscal policy', National Bureau of Economic Research Working Paper No. 17, 344.

III

Targets and Instruments

6   The MPC Remit at 25: Growing Pains?

Jens Larsen

On 6 May 1997, five days after the 1997 General Election, Chancellor Gordon Brown sent a letter to Governor Eddie George setting out the new framework for monetary policy. That was followed up on 12 June with a further letter entitled 'Remit for the MPC'.[1] Together, the two letters clearly defined the objectives of Monetary Policy Committee (MPC) and gave a steer on how to manage the inevitable trade-offs. It was a clear statement of delegation from the government to the MPC that also specified an accountability framework. The remit letter has been an important feature of the UK monetary policy framework since then.[2,3]

This chapter is divided into two parts. First, I will provide a brief review of the first remit and why it would come to play such a key role in defining the monetary policy framework in the early years of the MPC. I will discuss why the same concept has worked less well in other contexts, drawing on the UK's attempts to introduce a remit for the International Monetary Fund (IMF) and pointing out the absence of a financial stability remit to match that for monetary policy.

With those experiences in mind, I will set out why the remit is still useful after the Global Financial Crisis (GFC), when the macroeconomic policy framework, and the Bank's role in it, has expanded reflecting the shortcomings that the GFC exposed. The risk of an overload of competing objectives is clear, however, with the primacy of the price stability objective at risk.

In the second part of the chapter, I will ask whether and to what extent the MPC's remit should be expanded further to include climate change. There is a strong argument that climate change and the policy response to it pose direct challenges to both the Bank's price and financial stability

---

[1] These and the following remit and minutes documents are readily available on the Bank of England website.

[2] For a full account of the discussion leading up to the Bank's independence see James (2020) and Kynaston (2017).

[3] The remit is mandated by Part 2, Section 12 of the Bank of England Act. Sections 11 and 12 set out the objectives.

objectives: the central bank hence has an obligation to address these challenges, whether climate change is mentioned in the remit or not. Arguably, the recent inclusion of climate change as a secondary objective provides direct democratic legitimacy to the central bank's involvement, which could be helpful when the MPC faces trade-offs.

A Time of Innocence, a Time of Confidences[4] – the First MPC Remit

Although the 12 June letter carries the title 'Remit for the MPC', it must be read with the 6 May letter, which covers more ground than just monetary policy, including reform of the Bank's Court, the Bank's financial affairs and the transitional arrangements to the new regime. The first self-contained remit is dated June 1998. This 1998 remit is a clear, concise and stand-alone document.

Over three pages, using only about 700 words, it sets out the framework for monetary policy in its entirety. The primary objective of monetary policy is to maintain price stability. The Bank is given a clearly subordinated objective of supporting the government's economic policy, subject to achieving its primary price stability objective. Price stability is operationalised through the inflation target, then 2.5% RPIX inflation. The remit also sets out a trade-off between inflation and output volatility. The two effectively define the MPC's preferences. The remit also specifies a mechanism to account for large deviations from the target in the form of a letter writing regime whereby the Governor would send a letter to the chancellor if a deviation from target of more than one percentage point occurs. Furthermore, it sets out an accountability framework, with the MPC being accountable for its monetary policy decisions to the government, to Parliament and to the public. Finally, the remit contains a pithy summary of the government's central economic objective as achieving high and stable levels of growth and employment. The contribution of price stability to achieving this objective is spelt out.

Curiously, in retrospect, there was no discussion of the policy instruments. In 1997, it was perhaps self-evident that monetary policy meant 'interest rates'. The minutes of the first meeting of the MPC in June 1997 state that the Committee members 'judged that a modest increase in interest rates was needed immediately', a proposition which was supported by all six members.

All in all, the 1998 remit was an exceptionally clear and self-contained document that made the UK monetary policy regime stand out for its

---

[4] Paul Simon, Bookends (1968).

clarity and coherence in comparison to other jurisdictions and in sharp contrast with the past. The remit provided a strong basis for a delegation of a significant public policy responsibility with a clear accountability framework, thereby underpinning the legitimacy of the new regime and overcoming long-standing concerns about the idea of delegating a critical macroeconomic policy tool.

For over a decade the remit was left largely unchanged, except for a practically inconsequential change of the target from 2.5% RPIX inflation to 2% CPI inflation in December 2003 and continued to be the main delegation mechanism until the GFC. The extensive debate in policy circles and academia about 'leaning against the wind', be it in the form of countering asset price or house price bubbles or taking financial stability into account, had no impact on the remit.

Are Remits a Universal Tool? Experiences from the IMF

Given the positive macroeconomic outcomes at the time, it is no wonder that there was a widespread pride in the regime within which the remit played such a key role. Not only did MPC members regularly sing its praise, the Treasury wrote a book about the macro policy framework (HM Treasury, 2001). The enthusiasm for the remit as a delegation and accountability tool was in fact so strong that it was considered a potential export item for other areas of economic policy and internationally.

An example of this was the UK's contribution to improving the quality and the traction of the IMF's bilateral and multilateral surveillance in the period after the 1997 Asian Financial Crisis. This was at a time where Gordon Brown held the chair of the influential International Monetary and Financial Committee (IMFC),[5] and the Bank and HM Treasury were very active in international financial policy. I am not sure exactly when the idea of a remit from the IMFC to the IMF management[6] was introduced, but it caused considerable opposition and consternation. In the end, it was not part of the surveillance framework that emerged from a long and contentious reform process. The ins and outs of that process are well beyond the scope of this chapter – in fact, it is the subject of a forthcoming volume on the evolution of the IMF's surveillance framework in the 21st century (Ghosh and Postelnyak, 2022).

---

[5] For those unfamiliar with the IMFC and its role, see www.imf.org/en/About/Factsheets/A-Guide-to- Committees-Groups-and-Clubs#IC. Gordon Brown was IMFC chair from 1999 to 2007.
[6] An early reference is Balls (2003).

Why is this failure relevant to a discussion of the MPCs remit? The IMF process demonstrated that the remit as a tool is by no means universal. In my view, the main issue was unclear governance arrangements: which of the many international committees and bodies had both the legal standing and political clout to provide a clear delegation to the IMF management and hold it to account?

That issue could not be resolved.[7] The absence of a clear intellectual framework, specific objectives and the well-defined policy tools would have made the drafting of a remit more arduous, but it was the lack of clear governance arrangements that made it impossible.

That insight might help us to understand why domestically, there was no remit for the Bank's financial stability mandate to match the remit on the monetary policy side. The absence of a clear and agreed intellectual framework probably played a role, but the fundamental governance issues with the tripartite arrangement were key in the failure to provide the clarity to financial stability that so clearly benefitted monetary policy. It took the GFC to change that with the first remit for the Financial Policy Committee (FPC) being issued in April 2013.

Innocence Lost: The Expansion of the MPC Remit

In 2013, the MPC remit was substantially expanded, reflecting the experience of the GFC and the profound rethink of the macroeconomic policy framework. The 2021 version, which I will take as a basis for my discussion, is longer (at close to 1,500 words plus a cover letter), uses more complex language and covers more ground than the 1998 remit.

This longer MPC remit sits alongside the remit for the FPC, coming in at 3,800 words and a long cover letter. It is also worth recalling that four of the five internal MPC members are members of the FPC (and of the Prudential Regulation Committee for that matter).

The core of the MPC remit remains the same, and the delegation and accountability framework is unchanged: the chancellor sets a target that operationalises the price stability objective and specifies trade-offs and how to deal with large inflation under- and overshoots; the remit establishes an accountability framework to the government, parliament and the public. But much else has changed, with several important expansions.

The 2021 remit is more explicit on trade-offs between output and inflation. It gives the MPC more flexibility to choose the pace at which

---

[7] It probably did not help that the concept of a remit was unfamiliar to many nor that the UK had followed a less-than-conventional approach in getting the IMFC to agree that it wanted a remit. See Ghosh and Postelnyak (2022), p. 151.

inflation is brought back to target. Financial stability risks are explicitly recognised: while the FPC is the 'first line of defence', the MPC is given a clear steer that it 'may wish to allow inflation to deviate from the target temporarily, consistent with its need to have regard to the policy actions of the FPC'. The co-ordination with the FPC is explicitly mandated, complete with a description of the accountability framework.

The 2021 remit also specifies the governance of 'unconventional policy instruments' and, in particular, clarifies that the MPC has an obligation to seek approval for such instruments – in addition to asset purchases that include tools that support the funding of commercial banks' balance sheets, such as the Funding for Lending Scheme. The MPC is free to decide on forward guidance, presumably because that is judged not to have financial consequences.[8]

Finally, the section on the government's economic policy objectives is substantially expanded, focusing on strong, sustainable and balanced growth. In addition to providing credible frameworks for monetary and fiscal policies, the government's strategy includes structural reforms to support 'levelling up' and the net-zero transition. It also includes maintaining a resilient, effectively regulated and competitive financial system to protect consumers, the taxpayer and – with a second mention – the net-zero transition.

On the whole, this is a significant expansion of the role of the MPC. The primary objective remains as stipulated by the Bank of England Act. However, the MPC has more flexibility in dealing with inflation deviations; more choice in terms of instruments, including some that directly affect the availability and cost of credit; a significant role in financial stability, even if it is secondary to the FPC; and finally, a much broader secondary objective including a double mention of the net-zero transition.

Some regret the loss of clarity of the remit: not only is it now too long and too complex for a non-technical audience to appreciate, but there is also a view that the expansion of the role of the MPC, and more generally of the Bank, poses substantial democratic challenges and ultimately threatens the Bank's independence and capacity to do well what only it can do: ensure price stability (Tucker, 2018).

While I have sympathy for those looking for a simpler world and certainly agree that an independent monetary policy is critical, I think it is a strength of the remit that it attempts to deal clearly with the complex challenges facing macroeconomic policymakers. That is not an invitation to overload the MPC or the Bank with objectives they have neither the

---

[8] The remit curiously still does not spell out what the conventional policy instrument is.

tools nor capacity to deal with. But the remit should reflect the reality that the MPC and the Bank now play significant roles in the allocation of liquidity, funding, capital and risk.

It would be wrong to pretend that these tools can be deployed in a 'neutral' fashion – these policy decisions clearly play an important role in the allocation of resources, and that allocation depends on what other policy steps the government might take. To my mind, it is much better to acknowledge and codify that influence, provide clear and limited objectives for the central bank, underpinned by an appropriate delegation and an accountability framework. That is the lesson of the GFC.

The risk, though, is clear: the primacy of the price stability objective may be undermined by an overload of subordinated objectives and competing policy concerns, particularly for those policymakers that wear multiple hats.

Should the Remit Include Climate Change?

Does the current remit strike the right balance? Given the already substantially expanded role of the MPC and the Bank, is it wise to also include climate change in the remit, and if so, how?

It is clear that the central bank will not be the principal economic policymaker in this area. Most would agree that the net-zero transition will require a substantial re-allocation of resources, using tax, investment and regulatory tools that properly lie with government. The MPC's remit should not be overloaded with a climate mandate in order to provide the government with an excuse for insufficient action (King, 2021). So far, so easy.

But the scale of the transition and the effect on macroeconomic outcomes are broad and will affect the MPC's ability to meet its primary objective. For this brief discussion, I would point to three important macroeconomic issues: first, large and persistent moves in relative prices as the cost of carbon emissions rises to achieve the necessary re-allocation of resources; second, a substantial initial rise in investment expenditure share at least in the next decade in order to support the green transition; finally, rising uncertainty and risk, associated with physical and transition risks.

It is beyond the scope of this short chapter to discuss these effects in any detail. But even at this superficial level, it is clear that the central bank's ability to achieve its objectives is going to be affected by these developments. It is also clear that the policy measures central banks take will matter.

This is perhaps most obvious in the financial stability sphere. If you accept the argument that there are physical and transition risks that could give rise to substantial financial losses, then climate change will likely have financial stability impact, and there is a strong argument for policy intervention.[9] The Bank has micro- and macroprudential policy tools that affect the allocation of risk and capital so it can respond to these risks as they would to others. It is thus hard to argue against climate change as a first-order concern in a financial stability context.

But what about monetary policy?[10] Even in the absence of secondary objectives, price stability is likely to be directly affected by climate change and policies that respond to it. Indeed, we need to look no further than the current dramatic rise in energy prices to see an instance where past energy policy decisions have contributed to increased energy price volatility that challenges low and stable inflation.

In broader terms, while climate change is not the principal driver of these current price stability concerns, it could well be the case in the future that a mix of physical climate outcomes and carbon reduction policies cause economic and price volatility. In addition, the shift in resources towards a higher investment share that the energy transition requires might increase the real interest rate associated with price stability (known affectionately as R^*) by increasing investment relative to available savings. And finally, more tail events – be it in terms of physical events or in terms of negative financial outcomes – might put downward pressure on R^* by increasing uncertainty and risk.

Given the potential importance of these effects, monetary policy should at the very least be climate aware – that is, a policy that takes effective account of the impact of climate change and climate change policies on achieving its primary objective.

Does that mean that it is unnecessary to include it as a secondary objective? Arguably, including it in the secondary objectives is helpful in that it provides a clear mandate. The Bank has already heeded that change in remit by giving its balance sheet policies a 'green tilt'.[11] That reflects what is now a widely held view in the academic literature that this is the appropriate course of action.[12] This may matter less now, where the MPC is on the cusp of disposing of its corporate bond portfolio. But

---

[9] There is now a large literature on this topic. The classical reference is Carney (2015).

[10] The European Central Bank's 2021 strategy review includes an extensive review of climate change. See: Drudi et al. (2021).

[11] See Bank of England (2021). This paper sets out how the Bank uses its balance sheet to incentivise bond issuers to support transition by adjusting the composition of Corporate Bond Purchase Scheme to support the net-zero transition in ways that will not compromise its monetary policy objectives.

[12] See Fisher (2021).

looking ahead, as a matter of consistency, it would surely make sense that purchases are conducted in a forward-looking manner, in line with the requirements that the Bank as a regulator imposes on banks and insurance companies, as opposed to a backward looking 'market neutrality' concept that reflects historic issuance. Even if the direct impact of such a decision is likely to be small, it would send the wrong signal not to acknowledge the role the Bank plays in the allocation of capital.

But does the secondary objective matter directly for monetary policy decisions? If the monetary policymakers were to care directly about emissions, then it could create a trade-off with output: it would mean a willingness to sacrifice growth and accept higher volatility, in return for more emission reduction through a reduction in output.[13]

What does that mean in practice? We will need a well-specified model to answer that question with any precision – it will depend critically on the trade-off between output and emissions and of course the weight the central bank puts on avoiding emissions now and in the future. Government policy will matter too. But to get a sense of the direction, consider the following thought experiment: if the government imposes a carbon tax that raises the price of carbon-intensive consumption, how should the central bank respond?[14]

If we accept that emission reduction is part of the objective function, then it would be wrong to act to fully offset that decline in consumption by easing monetary policy. First order, the right reaction would be to act as if this were any other supply shock: monetary policy should act to ensure that the increase in some prices is offset by the decline in others over time. It should, on the usual mantra, avoid second-round effects on inflation dynamics.

However, if emission reduction is part of the objective, you could argue the central bank should act more aggressively – because the reduction in emissions that comes from lower output makes an output deviation less costly, and because the higher real interest rate shifts resources away from consumption towards investment. If, on top of that, the government is able to redistribute the proceeds and raise investments, then the argument for higher real interest rates becomes stronger (Schnabel, 2022). There are clearly limits to that argument: including climate change as a secondary objective for the Bank does not require it to cause a recession

---

[13] This is similar to the sustainable finance literature, where some argue that the traditional focus on returns and volatility should be extended to a third dimension, for example sustainability or impact. It seems reasonable to argue that at least in the short run, there could be a trade-off between impact and expected returns.

[14] The optimal policy response will clearly depend on the policy action taken by the government (Papoutsi, Piazzesi and Schneider, 2021).

to get emissions down or to deter consumption. Nevertheless, it does establish a trade-off.

That may feel like taking things a step too far at this point. I think the argument will become stronger over time, as it becomes clearer that we are behind when it comes to achieving the required emission reductions and the impact on the economy and markets becomes more pronounced. The presence of climate change in the remit may help the MPC anticipate these developments and act early.

Conclusion

The first MPC remit was a critical innovation in the UK macroeconomic policy framework, providing a clear delegation from government and strong accountability, underpinned by a simple and clear intellectual framework. The remit has stood the test of time, in my view principally because of the clarity of the delegation and accountability framework, rather than the simple intellectual underpinning, specific objectives and the well-defined policy tools. In fact, even when it turned out that the intellectual underpinnings were inadequate and the macroeconomic policy framework was substantially redesigned with a broader role for the MPC and with the addition of a comprehensive macroprudential framework, the remit has retained an important role.

In principle, the remit does not need to be expanded further to include climate change as an objective because the physical and transition risks associated with climate change affect the primary objective. However, in practice it is helpful for the MPC that the delegation explicitly mentions climate change, particularly when the Committee inevitably faces trade-offs.

References

Balls, Edward (2003), 'Preventing financial crises: The case for independent IMF surveillance', Remarks made at the Institute for International Economics, Washington, DC, 6 March.

Bank of England (2021), 'Options for greening the Bank of England's Corporate Bond Purchase Scheme', Discussion Paper, Bank of England.

Carney, Mark (2015), 'Breaking the tragedy of the horizon–climate change and financial stability'. Speech given at Lloyd's of London, 29 September, 220–30.

Drudi, Francesco, Emanuel Moench, Cornelia Holthausen et al. (2021), 'Climate change and monetary policy in the euro area', Occasional Paper Series No. 271, European Central Bank.

Fisher, Paul (2021), 'Greening the central bank balance sheet, or not?' Central Banking. [online] www.centralbanking.com/central-banks/governance/7873141/greening-the-central-bank-balance-sheet-or-not [Accessed 19 February 2022].

Ghosh, Atish and Anna Postelnyak (2022), The IMF in the Twenty-First Century – Surveillance Milestones I: The 2007 Surveillance Decision. IMF, forthcoming.

HM Treasury (2001), *Reforming Britain's Economic and Financial Policy: Towards Greater Economic Stability*, Springer.

James, Harold (2020), *Making of Modern Central Bank, the Bank of England 1979–2003*, Cambridge University Press.

King, Mervyn (2021), House of Lords Debate, 12 March, Lords Chamber, Vol. 810.

Kynaston, David (2017), *The Time's Last Sand – A History of the Bank of England 1694–2013*, Bloomsbury.

Papoutsi, Melina, Monika Piazzesi and Martin Schneider (2021), 'How unconventional is green monetary policy'. JEEA-FBBVA Lecture at the ASSA.

Schnabel, Isabel (2022), 'Looking through higher energy prices? Monetary policy and the green transition'. Remarks at the American Finance Association 2022 Virtual Annual Meeting.

Simon, Paul (1968), Bookends.

Tucker, Paul (2018), *Unelected Power*, Princeton University Press.

7   Raising the Inflation Target

Tony Yates

Introduction

Much ink has been spilled on the issue of how to design central bank mandates since the improvised and hasty birth of the inflation target in the UK in the aftermath of its exit from Europe's Exchange Rate Mechanism in the autumn of 1992. This chapter is a brief introduction to the argument for raising the inflation target in the light of the experience since the target was first set and aims to spill as little further ink as possible.[1]

It is worth saying that mandates should not be changed at will. The monetary policy mandate and the mechanisms for holding the central bank accountable for its performance in achieving it are meant to tie down expectations of the central bank's future behaviour, which in turn is key for anchoring inflation expectations and achieving monetary policy objectives. If mandates are changed frequently and discretionarily, current promises encoded in the mandate will not be expected to hold in the future.

At the same time, monetary policy choices will not be expected to endure if there is not a consensus among political actors and society at large that they are the right choices. If the evidence about the optimal mandate changes, but the mandate does not, people may not believe policies aimed at pursuing the old mandate, and eventually a change may be forced. Central bank mandates – and their durability – are means to other ends, not ends in themselves.

In the UK, what level of inflation to target is a decision reserved for the government and the Treasury. The Bank has operational independence with respect to the conduct of monetary policy. The goals of monetary policy remain directly in the hands of the elected government. This division of labour is optimal. It is not good for the central bank to set the target and make the operational policy decisions to hit the target: such

---

[1] These remarks recapitulate to some extent arguments put forward on my blog and twitter feed, in a written submission to Treasury Committee, and interventions with others, including James Smith and Richard Barwell, whom I thank without implicating in any errors made here.

an arrangement has the appearance of giving an incentive to manipulate the target so that the policy looks well executed. Furthermore, in a democracy, it is desirable to delegate as few powers as possible to technocratic institutions removed from political accountability.

In this chapter, I shall first provide the context in which the UK's current inflation target was initially introduced. I shall then review the macroeconomic developments since the target was set and the resulting challenges – most notably, the zero lower bound on nominal interest rates. Unconventional policy measures to maintain price stability and stimulate the economy at the zero lower bound will then be discussed. Finally, the drawbacks of raising the inflation target will be considered and conclusions drawn.

History and Motivation for the 2% Inflation Target

The UK inflation target of 2%, as measured by the twelve-month increase in the Consumer Price Index, dates back to the inflation target's inception in 1992, before the Bank was made independent in 1997.[2] The UK's target was set in haste in the chaotic economic and political aftermath of the UK's exit from the Exchange Rate Mechanism in Europe. There was no particular science in its choice. First, in its nature and quantification it resembled targets chosen by Canada and New Zealand. Second, it was a nominal anchor that we had not yet failed at (previous failures being the Gold Standard, exchange rate targeting, and money targeting).

Later, the central banking community as a whole ex-post-rationalised the consensus figure of 2% as the optimal rate, weighing up various factors. On the one hand, the arguments in favour of a relatively low inflation target included the Friedman rule, which prescribes setting the inflation rate equal to minus the equilibrium real rate of interest in order to equate the risk-adjusted real returns to holding money and other assets, as well as the existence of menu costs of changing prices, which are minimised at an inflation rate of zero. On the other hand, the factors supporting a higher inflation target encompassed the presence of upward biases in the inflation index rooted in the arrival of new goods, new outlets and quality improvements,[3] which may lead to official measures

---

[2] Although the initial target was 1–4%, with a midpoint of 2.5%, it was set in terms of RPIX inflation, which at the time was judged to be on average about 0.5 percentage points higher than CPI inflation. Therefore, the initial target of 2.5% in terms of RPIX growth and the current target of 2% in terms of CPI growth can be considered to be equivalent.

[3] On the debate about how best to combat biases in the CPI, see the original Boskin Commission report (Boskin et al., 1996), and a retrospective ten years later by Gordon (2006).

overstating actual inflation, and the existence of downward nominal stickiness in wages and perhaps prices, which might hinder wage and price adjustment if the inflation target is set too low. Finally, a key argument for setting the target at a higher level is the possibility that a shock might arrive – as indeed it did – that would force the central bank to lower the policy rate to its floor, of approximately zero, rendering conventional monetary policy tools ineffective. The lower bound on nominal interest rates exists because market rates cannot be tempted below a rate equal to zero less the cost of the storage, management and security of cash, as at that point investors have the possibility to store wealth in cash, which earns a more competitive rate. The lower the inflation target, the higher the risk of the policy rate hitting its floor.

Economic News since the 2% Target Was Set

Relative to that period in the early to mid-1990s, what have we learned? There have been some improvements to the way consumer price indices are collected, which have reduced the upward bias in measured inflation. The spread of digital technologies has probably reduced the costs of collecting information about the optimal price, and in reposting prices, lowering menu costs and thus detaching the optimal inflation rate somewhat from the zero inflation ideal. If there were significant downward nominal wage and price rigidities, then a couple of decades of low inflation may have eroded that somewhat, provided that the prior source of that rigidity was the lack of precedent for actual nominal wage cuts in an era of high inflation.[4]

The other evidence we have accumulated relates to the precise location of the interest rate floor, which may be somewhat lower than we first thought. Several countries experimented with the central bank rate below zero, without great ill effects; the UK revised down its estimate of the lower bound on nominal interest rates from an initial guess of 0.5% to 0.1%. This experience diminishes a little the need to accommodate the interest rate floor in the choice of the inflation target.

Of much greater significance, however, is that we have learned that we are much more likely to encounter the interest rate floor than we thought and to spend more time with rates trapped at that lower bound.

Japan first hit the zero bound to interest rates at the end of 1995 and has remained there ever since.[5] Japan's financial crisis at the beginning of the

[4] See, for example, Dickens et al. (2007) but also Elsby (2009).
[5] For a brief review of the early experience at the zero bound, see, for example, Dudley (2013).

1990s, which precipitated that experience, was – I think – deemed by the policy community outside Japan to be something that was special to the country's political-economic circumstances and not likely to be replicated in Western economies, and so not something we needed to use the monetary policy regime to guard against. The events that began in 2008 caused those who held this view to revise it. The UK interest rate hit what it determined was the floor first in March 2009 and did not make a first move above the revised estimate of the floor until December 2021.

Regulatory reform in the UK and elsewhere ensued, including measures to strengthen both the asset (with capital requirements) and liabilities (with liquidity regulation) side of banks' balance sheets. A new resolution regime was instituted to allow the authorities to seize and wind up troubled banks. A new Financial Policy Committee (FPC) was set up. It undertook to conduct macroprudential policy, adjusting prudential tools as the business cycle and financial conditions evolved. These reforms may have done something to mitigate the risk of a repeat of the 2008 Global Financial Crisis (GFC). Nevertheless, greater risk probably remains, relative to perceptions before the crisis itself, and a zero bound episode is all the more likely just because of the post-crisis legacy of very low equilibrium real interest rates. Moreover, the Covid-19 pandemic and the Russian invasion of Ukraine have reminded us that large shocks can emanate from other sources.

The Inflation Target and the Fisher Relation

Other things equal, a natural response to these developments is to raise the inflation target. The effect of this, eventually, would be to raise the resting point for central bank rates, roughly one for one, thus making room for larger cuts to central bank rates without hitting the interest rate floor. Why and how the room gets made is encoded in the Fisher effect, the theoretical version of which explains that investors holding a risk-free nominal bond will want to be compensated for the expected depreciation of the nominal bond brought about by higher inflation and will thus offer a lower price for the bond, which corresponds to a higher nominal interest rate. A higher inflation target thus, if credible, raises expectations of inflation and raises the interest rate eventually.

There are those who subscribe to 'neo-Fisherite' views, who would not accept the need for raising the inflation target. According to these views, the reason inflation undershoots the target is not because the lower bound is preventing interest rates from falling enough but because interest rates are low and expected to be so. These views correspond to certain equilibria in the New Keynesian model, but they are based on the strong assumption of rational expectations and conflict with empirical evidence on the impact of identified monetary policy shocks, so I view them as an intellectual curioso.[6]

Alternative Policy Tools

Against this backdrop and as a consequence of encountering the zero bound, policymakers have been forced to stimulate the economy with alternative instruments. The case for raising the inflation target to make more room for further cuts in interest rates rests on the efficacy of the alternatives, including quantitative easing (QE), policies aimed at managing interest rate expectations, fiscal policy instruments and reforms of the use of cash.

Quantitative Easing

In the wake of the GFC, many central banks resorted to QE as an unconventional policy measure in order to stimulate the economy. Central bank asset purchases, which in the UK totalled £895bn,[7] have their own difficulties that make them less than a perfect substitute for interest rate changes.[8] Although there is now a large literature demonstrating that such asset purchases have affected the prices and yields of the corresponding assets, at least to me it remains controversial what caused those changes, whether they were durable and whether they would be replicated outside of financial crisis-like periods.[9] That these purchases involved creating new electronic money, buying largely government-issued securities, and holding them for a very long period made them look hard to distinguish from monetary financing. This threatens to undermine the separation of monetary and fiscal policy.

Quantitative easing gave birth to political hostility. One manifestation of this was the proposal of 'People's Quantitative Easing', supported for a time by Jeremy Corbyn during his September 2015 campaign for the Labour Party leadership, and which proposed to requisition QE to be directed at favoured public works or causes, implicitly criticising QE as

---

[6] See, for example, Williamson (2016) for a supportive account of the neo-Fisherian proposal; also, see Cochrane (2016).

[7] See Bank of England, for example the introduction to 'Quantitative Easing' on the Bank's website.

[8] See, for example, then external Monetary Policy Committee member Vlieghe (2019) remarking that asset purchases are imperfect substitutes for interest rate policy, p. 10.

[9] For a survey supportive of QE, see Gagnon (2016); for a more sceptical view, see Martin and Milas (2012) and Williamson (2017).

sending funds somehow to those other than 'the people'.[10] Another manifestation of disquiet at QE was the argument holding it responsible for inflating asset prices – a feature, in fact, and not a bug – and increasing inequality. That in turn has fuelled debate about whether the central bank should be tasked with targeting inequality, presumably with the intention of forcing it to temper its resort to asset purchases. Without addressing that critique (highly contestable) or the policy prescription (a bad idea) in any detail, it is worth noting that without QE such arguments would not have arisen.[11]

Other drawbacks of asset purchases have also been discussed: that they distort and shrink the market for liquid collateral; that they may conflict with and complicate debt management (crudely, the debt management office may have an incentive to issue into the habitats of the debt market that have high prices, pushing them down, while the central bank is trying to push those prices up and yields down); that private sector asset purchases expose the central bank to political and reputational risk (appearing to favour the issuers, the costs of being observed to buy assets on which the central bank subsequently loses money).

Managing Interest Rate Expectations

Another alternative to cutting interest rates at the floor is to rely on manipulating expectations of future interest rates. In the canonical New Keynesian model, optimal policy under rational expectations and commitment has the property that the closer a shock threatens to take rates towards the interest rate floor, the more the policy response implies a disproportionately large and protracted interest rate cut ('lower for longer') and corresponding inflation overshooting the target afterwards.[12] The difficulty with implementing the policy is convincing people that the central bank will follow through with the inflation overshoot once the threat of deflation and the zero bound has passed. Once you have manipulated interest rate expectations downwards and inflation expectations upwards and have reaped the benefit of the fall in real rates, boosting spending and thus inflation itself, there is an incentive to renege later on and avoid a costly inflation overshoot. Even if policymakers were sufficiently determined, observers in the economy may not be sophisticated or forward-looking enough to attend to what the central bank is communicating.

---

[10] For a description of and comment on 'People's Quantitative Easing' see Yates (2015).

[11] A counter might be that even without QE, the effects of very low natural real interest rates which were ascribed to QE would have generated the same opprobrium.

[12] See, for example, Eggertsson and Woodford (2003); result prefigured in Krugman (1998).

The Fed's flexible average inflation target (FAIT) can be viewed as an attempt to implement this forward guidance policy insofar as it commits policy to compensate for inflation undershoots, induced by the missing stimulus at the interest rate floor, with subsequent overshoots.[13]

Reviewing the FAIT deserves a paper on its own. But suffice it to say that I think the framework is highly problematic. It introduces a new intermediate target in pursuit of the ultimate objective, which is confusing. And it is ambiguous. It does not specify a horizon over which any average is to be computed and thus does not clearly tie down the inflation overshoot to the undershoot.

The US is clearly experiencing a large overshoot, with inflation running at 7.9% at the time of writing. Ironically, its credibility may be suffering not because of a failure to follow through and generate an overshoot but a failure to generate one small enough. The overshoot is bound up with the peculiar effects of Covid-19 – the lockdown policies, voluntary social distancing and the fiscal response. What lessons Fed observers will carry forward to the next zero bound episode is not clear.

Fiscal Instruments

Conventional fiscal tools – by which I mean the array of spending and tax instruments commonly used by a country's finance ministry – are relatively more costly to move around, may be slower to adjust in some cases – particularly with regard to spending – and using them interferes with other government objectives, such as pay policy, policy towards public investment and business. At the point when these fiscal instruments need to be used, they also reverse the delegation intended when inflation targets and central bank independence were instigated and motivated by an attempt to insulate monetary and macroeconomic policies from the electoral cycle.

Reform of the Use of Cash

A final alternative to raising the inflation target is to make the necessary reforms in order to permit interest rates to fall a great deal below the current floor. The way to eliminate the floor altogether is to abolish cash altogether. In a world with no cash, if the central bank sets negative interest rates, private banks can set their rates negative and depositors will not withdraw their funds, as there is no zero-interest-rate alternative to beat the depreciating deposits. Short of abolition, there are options to

---

[13] See Powell (2020) on the FAIT.

make cash less attractive by eliminating higher denominations (meaning that you need more notes to store a given amount of wealth), the effect of which would be to lower the interest rate floor somewhat. Such options have the coincidental benefit of taxing those using cash for nefarious means, either for tax evasion or illegal trade. These proposals have a long pedigree, relating back to Gesel (1891) who proposed cash that expired, thus entailing a negative interest rate, which would allow market rates to be significantly negative.

I am against going down this route any further than that needed to address illicit use of cash. First, there are arguments (see, e.g., Cochrane, 2015) that people may invent cash substitutes or use alternative existing means such as other states' cash, or digital monies or prepayment cards. Second, abolishing cash would require providing a state, digital and taxable alternative, not in itself a decisive argument against, but we are not there yet. Third, it is not as realistic a political possibility as raising the inflation target, and it is not clear to me that it could be easily sold or explained as a policy initiative without generating fear and confusion.

The Drawbacks of a Higher Inflation Target

There are several drawbacks to raising the inflation target: the costs of the extra inflation generated; the danger of inducing indeterminacy; the risks that policy effectiveness will diminish, that high inflation necessarily means more variable inflation and that a target change would undermine the credibility of monetary policy.

There are competing factors weighing on the optimal inflation rate. Raising it requires that the benefits – in terms of the room generated for more interest rate cuts and less reliance on alternative instruments – outweigh the costs.

One risk identified in the New Keynesian literature on monetary policy is that higher inflation generates more possibility for price-level indeterminacy; specifically, higher inflation narrows the range of model parameters for which interest rates rules eliminate it.[14] This consideration does not weigh heavily in my view because it is a pathology of rational expectations models, a knife-edge result which would not be obtained if the world departs even a small distance from rational expectations.

A second drawback to note, related to the previous one, is that it is possible that as the inflation target increases, inducing a corresponding increase in the average inflation rate, the effectiveness of policy diminishes. This might come about because the higher inflation induces more

---

[14] This risk is explained in Ascari and Sbordonne (2014) and Kara and Yates (2021).

frequent price changes. This would have the effect of 'using up' some of the room generated via the Fisher effect, as policy would have to respond to shocks more vigorously.

Third, it has been contended that higher inflation necessarily means more variable inflation. This correlation exists in the data across countries and regimes.[15] However, aside from the indeterminacy argument, there is no good theoretical reason for this correlation to be inevitable. The correlation in the data is most likely due to the fact that the higher inflation regimes experienced are simply the ones where there is poor monetary policy design and conduct. This institutional and policy dysfunction lead both to higher and more variable inflation. There is no historical precedent for attempting to choose to conduct sound inflation and real economic stability at higher rates of inflation.

A fourth drawback is that there are difficulties in going from the existing target to the higher one. If inflation starts below target, and if interest rates are trapped at their floor, it may be hard to achieve a higher inflation target. Pre-announcing a higher target may simply set up the central bank for more dramatic failure. If inflation is above target – as it is now – announcing a higher target may look to some like a cynical ploy to avoid bringing inflation back under control. Either way, agents in the economy need to be given some warning so that the target change does not have the quasi-expropriating effects associated with surprise inflations.

Partly to guard against cynical interpretations of an inflation target change, the inflation target increase ought to emerge not as a fait accomplis but from a new process that commits to five-yearly reviews, which in principle would not rule out reversing the change later on if the evidence justified it, and the forces that pushed the target up in the first place had been shown to have gone into reverse.

Conclusions

In this chapter I have made the argument for a modest increase in the inflation target. Elsewhere, I and others have proposed a new target of 4% (see, for example, Blanchard, Dell'Ariccia and Mauro, 2010; Wren-Lewis, 2012; Krugman, 2013; Ball, 2013). The point of raising the target is to address the increased risk – evidenced by recent experience – of protracted periods during which interest rates are trapped at their floor, relative to perceptions of this risk at the time the 2% target was set in the early/mid-1990s. I have not in this discussion offered any real consideration of

---

[15] Early examples in this literature, which generated many more papers, are Okun (1971) and Gordon (1971).

precisely what the increase in the target should be. That probably needs a paper all of its own. The 200-basis point increase in room for rate cuts that the target change would generate (optimistically) is unlikely to be enough to respond fully. For that reason, further recourse to central bank asset purchases will be needed, alongside other institutional reforms.

While this chapter focuses on the inflation target, I do not think that reform should stop there. I believe that it would be beneficial to introduce a number of further changes to the monetary policy framework. First, the inflation target should be formalised as a dual mandate, and the 'subject to' clause included in the Remit that refers to stabilising the real economy should be eliminated.[16] Second, the Bank should be allowed to invite the Treasury to design a fiscal stimulus in the vicinity of the floor to interest rates in order to make up for the interest rate cuts it would like to have made, with the Office for Budget Responsibility assessing any plan HM Treasury devise for sustainability. Third, the increase in the target should not be permanent but should emerge from a process beginning regular five-year reviews, to assess how forces weighing on the optimal inflation target have evolved. However, the discussion of these reforms goes beyond the scope of the chapter.

References

Ascari, Guido and Argia Sbordonne (2014), 'The macroeconomics of trend inflation', *Journal of Economic Literature*. 52(3), 679–739.

Ball, Laurence (2013), 'The case for four per cent inflation', *Central Bank Review*. 13, 17–31.

Blanchard, Oliver, Giovanni Dell'Ariccia and Paolo Mauro (2010), 'Rethinking macroeconomic policy', IMF Staff Position Note, SPN/10/03, 12 February.

Boskin, Michael, Ellen Dulberger, Robert Gordon, Zvi Griliches and Dale Jorgenson (1996), 'Toward a more accurate measure of the cost of living'. Final report to the Senate Finance Committee.

Cochrane, John (2015), 'Cancel currency?' *The Grumpy Economist, blog*, 30 December 2014.

Cochrane, John (2016), 'Do higher interest rates raise or lower inflation?' BFI Working Paper.

Dickens, William, Lorenz Goette, Erica Groshen et al. (2007), 'How wages change: Micro evidence from the International Wage Flexibility Project', *Journal of Economic Perspectives*. 21(2), 195–214.

Dudley, William (2013), 'Lessons at the zero bound: The Japanese and U.S. experience', Speech 105, Federal Reserve Bank of New York.

---

[16] I say 'formalise' because I think in practice this is how it works already; a point made by the 'Review of the monetary policy framework' conducted by the Treasury itself in 2013, when it described the UK regime as one of 'flexible inflation targeting'.

Eggertsson, Gauti and Michael Woodford (2003), 'The zero bound on interest rates and optimal monetary policy', *Brookings Papers on Economic Activity.* 34(1), 139–235.

Elsby, Michael (2009), 'Evaluating the economic significance of downward nominal wage rigidity', *Journal of Monetary Economics.* 56(2), 154–69.

Gagnon, Joseph (2016), 'Quantitative Easing: An underappreciated success', Peterson Institute for International Economics, Policy Brief 16–4.

Gesel, Silvio (1891), *Currency Reform as a Bridge to the Social State.* Translated Philip Pye. Transcript. 1951.

Gordon, Robert (1971), 'Steady anticipated inflation: Mirage or oasis', *Brookings Papers on Economic Activity.* 2, 499–510.

Gordon, Robert (2006), 'The Boskin Commission Report: A retrospective one decade later', NBER Working Paper No. 12311.

Kara, Engin and Tony Yates (2021), 'A case against a 4 per cent inflation target', *Journal of Money, Credit and Banking.* 53(5), 1097–119.

Krugman, Paul (1998), 'It's baack: Japan's slump and the return of the liquidity trap', *Brookings Papers on Economic Activity.* 29(2), 137–206.

Krugman, Paul (2013), 'The four percent solution', *New York Times*, 24 May.

Martin, Christopher and Costas Milas (2012), 'Quantitative easing – A skeptical survey', *Oxford Review of Economic Policy.* 28(4), 750–64.

Okun, Arthur (1971), 'The mirage of steady inflation', *Brookings Papers on Economic Activity.* 2(2), 485–98.

Powell, Jerome (2020), 'New economic challenges and the Fed's monetary policy review'. Speech at an economic policy symposium sponsored by the Federal Reserve Bank of Kansas City, Jackson Hole, Wyoming, 27 August.

Rogoff, Kenneth (2016), *The Curse of Cash*, Princeton University Press.

Taylor, John (1981), 'On the relation between the variability of inflation and the average inflation rate', *Carnegie-Rochester Conference Series on Public Policy.* 15, 57–85.

Vlieghe, Gertjan (2019), 'Monetary policy: Adapting to a changed world', Bank of England, speech at the 2019 MMF Monetary and Financial Policy Conference, Bloomberg, London, 15 October.

Williamson, Stephen (2016), 'Neo-Fisherism: A radical idea, or the most obvious solution to the low-inflation problem?' *The Regional Economist*, Federal Reserve Bank of St. Louis, issue July, number 4–9.

Williamson, Stephen (2017), 'Quantitative easing: How well does this tool work?' *The Regional Economist*, Federal Reserve Bank of St. Louis, 25(3), 8–14.

Wren-Lewis, Simon (2012), 'The UK needs monetary policy to be as expansionary as possible and this isn't going to happen under the current system', LSE blog, 4 December.

Yates, Tony (2014), Submission for Treasury Committee inquiry on the 'effectiveness and impact of post-2008 monetary policy'.

Yates, Tony (2015), 'Corbyn's QE for the people jeopardises the Bank of England's independence', *Guardian*, 22 September.

8   What Have We Learnt about Unconventional Monetary Policy Tools? Lessons from the Global Pandemic

Charlotta Groth

As societies shut down in 2020, central banks re-deployed unconventional policy tools from the Global Financial Crisis (GFC) but also added new and even less conventional ones. The steps they took followed a textbook description of a risk management approach to monetary policy when operating close to the effective lower bound on interest rates.[1] This involved loosening policy aggressively and working with many different instruments simultaneously to maximise policy impact. Judging from the aftermath, they were successful. They steered the economy through a crisis and avoided a depression. One could argue that the episode has shown that monetary policy can be effective also in a low interest rate environment if central banks are willing and able to deploy multiple measures with scale and speed. This suggests that central banks are well equipped for the future, irrespective of the path of interest rates.

This chapter discusses some caveats to this conclusion, including the complementary fiscal measures, the effectiveness of forward guidance and shifting incentives during the exit process. There are also risks associated with the aggressive policy approach. Since the root cause of the effective lower bound on interest rate is the issuance of paper currency, the development of Central Bank Digital Currency (CBDC) offers a potential solution to the problem and could allow for a return to more conventional monetary policy.

This Time Is Different – Central Banks Did Not Act Alone

While monetary support measures were powerful during the pandemic, central banks did not act alone. Governments mobilised massive amounts of public funds to manage the health and economic crises. During the

---

[1] For an overview, see Evans et al. (2015). The risk management approach implies that central banks that operate in a low interest rate environment should respond more aggressively to economic conditions to reduce the risk associated with the effective lower bound on interest rates. This result relies on unconventional balance sheet tools being imperfect substitutes for the traditional policy rate.

pandemic's first year, discretionary measures to households and businesses reached 16% of GDP for the OECD countries.[2] Fiscal measures were directly targeted to households and businesses and involved a transfer from the government to the private sector. Central banks supported the fiscal expansion by holding down government borrowing costs through asset purchases, absorbing a large part of new debt issuance. Fiscal injections meant that resources quickly reached the real economy and led to a surge in broad money. The money multiplier did not collapse in contrast to the last crisis. Without complementary fiscal support, monetary policy actions would have been less potent.[3] In future crisis, the fiscal complementarity may not be as forthcoming.

The Power of Forward Guidance Can Be Eroded

Forward guidance was another component of policy that was relied on. Central banks made bold projections about how long they planned to keep support measures in place. In September 2020, the Federal Reserve provided outcome-based forward guidance indicating that an accommodative stance would be maintained until inflation had risen to 2% and was on track to moderately exceed 2% for some time. For the Fed, that was an unprecedented policy move. At that time, the median projection in the Fed's dot plot implied that rates would be kept unchanged until after 2023. The Bank of England (Bank) and the European Central Bank (ECB) made similar commitments, promising that policy would not be tightened until inflation had sustainably reached the 2% target. In August 2020, the Bank's Monetary Policy Committee projection, which was conditioned on a policy rate that remained close to 0% until the end of 2023, showed inflation only gradually approaching the 2% target over the same time horizon.

With the benefit of hindsight, forward guidance was too ambitious. But ex ante it was effective, as it helped to reduce policy uncertainty and strengthen the impact on long-term interest rates and broader financial conditions.[4]

This illustrates one of the problems with forward guidance. In the depth of a crisis, it is easy for policymakers to signal that support will remain in place for an extended period (cheap talk). But if measures are successful and the economy recovers, they will eventually have an

---

[2] OECD (2021).

[3] See Chadha et al. (2021) on the Covid-19 crisis and Bartsch et al. (2020) for a general discussion.

[4] Martinez-Garcia and Doehr (2022) and Bernanke (2020) provide empirical assessments of forward guidance.

incentive to scale back stimulus irrespective of past guidance. This is an example of the well-known time inconsistency problem.

Forward guidance exposes central banks to different forms of reputation risk. If the public fails to understand the conditionality of guidance, central bank credibility and their ability to influence expectations may over time become eroded, particularly if guidance is frequently and substantially revised. In the next crisis, forward guidance may not be as impactful, and more exotic guidance may be required to influence expectations. The offset is that central banks may need to do even more in future, if promises and guidance become less ineffective.

Exiting Will Always Be Disruptive

This leads on to and is closely linked to the removal of accommodation. The risk management approach to exiting from unconventional policies implies that accommodation should only be cautiously removed as risk remains asymmetric and to the downside. More uncertain policy instruments (asset purchases) should be removed first, and the policy rate should be left in place for longer.[5] To anchor expectations, central banks could condition one policy instrument (policy rate) on another (asset purchases), emphasising the sequencing of the two with a time lag built into the process. The purpose of this complicated approach is to build inertia into the process and avoid sharp and disruptive adjustments to interest rates and asset prices.

The approach has been adopted by central banks. The Bank stated that it would keep the stock of asset purchases unchanged until the Bank Rate had reached 0.5%. The stock would initially be reduced by ceasing reinvestments but, once the policy rate had reached 1%, the Bank could consider actively selling assets. Any unwinding of the stock of asset purchases was intended to move along 'a gradual and entirely predictable path'.[6] The Fed and the ECB adopted similar approaches.

Since these plans were initially published, the process of removing stimulus has been compressed as inflation has resurfaced. The Bank is furthest ahead and reached the 0.5% threshold already in February 2022, much earlier than expected when the quantitative easing (QE) withdrawal plan was first announced in August 2021.

It is too early to tell whether accommodation is removed too rapidly. Maybe this time is different. One observation though is that the risk management approach provides more consistent policy guidance when

---

[5] Evans (2015).
[6] For guidance and discussion, Bank of England (2021) and Financial Times (2021).

the economy is entering a recession compared to when it is exiting. At that point in time, a cautious approach to exiting (motivated by the asymmetry around the effective lower bound) is unlikely to be aligned with the incentives of policymakers who rightly focus on the risk of inflation. An average inflation targeting approach could help in this respect, as it tilts the incentives of policymakers in the direction of keeping stimulus in place for longer.[7] While an average inflation targeting approach has been adopted by the Fed, there appears to be limited appetite for this elsewhere, particularly against the backdrop of current elevated inflation.

A Moderate and Considerate Approach Is No Longer Optimal

When operating close to the effective lower bound, a moderate and considerate approach to monetary policy is not optimal. Instead, policymakers should aim at responding aggressively to events as, in that situation, inflation is preferred to deflation and policy space is restricted. But by reducing the risk of running out of policy space, this approach raises the risk of over-stimulating the economy if underlying economic conditions turn out to be less dire.

One potential side effect of a risk management approach to monetary policy is therefore a more volatile business cycle, where recessions are followed by sharp recoveries and where expectations of similar large-scale policy support in future crises encourage excessive risk taking in the real economy and financial markets.[8] As a result, this could amplify volatility in financial markets and the real economy, potentially limiting the ability of central banks to deliver on their broader mandate to provide economic and financial stability. The approach additionally assumes that there is no cost to raising rates quickly if needed. There are arguments for smoothing and gradualism that could delay the response to a potential overshoot and further amplify business cycle volatility.[9]

The Use of Multiple Instruments Challenges Central Bank Independence

Some argue that central banks have overstepped their mandate given the scope and the focus of unconventional monetary policy. Institutional arrangements are in many cases in place for the government to recapitalise

[7] For example, Curdia (2022).
[8] For a recent discussion, see English, Forbes and Ubide, (2021).
[9] Saunders (2018) discusses this in the context of Bank policy.

central banks should losses on their balance sheet operations materialise, which implies that monetary policy has direct fiscal implications. Asset purchases have additionally been shown to have important distributional consequences and may involve decisions around the allocation of credit. Should low interest rates persist and central banks continue to work with multiple instruments, their independence may over time become challenged, particularly if losses arise or if balance sheet operations involve risk assets.[10] Central bank independence should not be taken as given and will only last as long as the public believe that the benefits outweigh costs. To ensure appropriate accountability, a focus on measures that bring advantages for all and clear communication around the costs and benefits seem important.[11]

The Problem with the Effective Lower Bound on Interest Rates

To sum up, while the current policy approach was successful in stabilising the global economy during the Covid-19 crisis, it has drawbacks. They primarily stem from the existence of the effective lower bound on interest rates which forces central banks to work with multiple instruments and deploy an aggressive approach to policy. Large-scale usage of the balance sheet also poses difficult questions around the legitimacy and fairness of monetary policy.

In the decade after the GFC, there was hope that the economic cycle would be sufficiently elongated to allow central banks to raise policy rates back to pre-crisis levels. There is now hope that a more favourable mix between monetary and fiscal measures, efforts to reposition economies for a net-zero future and a stronger inflationary backdrop will help to drive equilibrium real and nominal interest rates higher.

Despite this, monetary policy is likely to remain constrained by the effective lower bound for the foreseeable future. In the seven rate-cutting cycles prior to the Covid-19 crisis, the Bank lowered the Bank Rate by over 400 bps on average. Even if measures to raise interest rates are successfully deployed, rebuilding this policy rate margin appears unlikely.

---

[10] The Bank of Japan, for example, is one of the largest investors in the Japanese exchange traded funds (ETF) market while the Swiss National Bank has 20% of its foreign currency reserves invested in global equity markets.

[11] For recent publications, see Dietch (2020) and Tucker (2018).

The Future of Paper Currency

The root cause of the effective lower bound on interest rate is the issuance of paper currency (cash), which effectively offers a zero nominal interest rate and therefore acts as an interest rate floor. It is well known that one way of getting rid of the effective lower bound would be to move towards a system where money is registered, for example in the form of being electronically issued.[12] Negative interest rates on deposits and bank balances could then be as easily implemented as positive interest rates.

While abandoning paper cash was unthinkable only a few years ago, most major central banks are now developing their own CBDC. Looking forward to the next 25 years, trends around CBDCs will likely be critical to whether central banks will continue to work with multiple instruments. If CBDCs become more widely adopted, it could allow for a return to conventional monetary policy with a focus on the short-term interest rate as the primary instrument.

This would be a positive development, given the advantages of the Bank Rate relative to less conventional balance sheet policies.[13] Should this development occur, a notable asymmetry in the design and implementation of monetary policy could be reduced. It would also have large-scale implications for interest rates, the savings industry and the financial sector more broadly.

References

Bank of England (2021), Monetary Policy Report, August.

Bartsch, Elga, Agnes Benassy-Quere, Gianluca Coresetti and Xavier Debrun (2020), 'It's all in the mix, how monetary and fiscal policies can work together or fail together', CEPR Press, no. 23.

Bernanke, Ben (2020), 'The new tools of monetary policy', American Economic Association Presidential Address, January.

Buiter, Willem (2009), 'Negative nominal interest rates: Three ways to overcome the zero lower bound', NBER Working Paper no. 15, 118.

Chadha, Jagjit, Luisa Corrado, Jack Meaning and Tobias Schuler (2021), 'Monetary and fiscal complementarity in the Covid-19 pandemic', ECB Working Paper Series, no. 2, 588.

Curdia, Vasco (2022), 'Average inflation targeting in the financial crisis recovery', *FRBSF Economic Letter*, January.

---

[12] See Buiter (2009) or, for a recent discussion, Vlieghe (2021).

[13] The policy rate is under the sole control of the central bank, it does not impact on the government's consolidated balance sheet, and its effects on the economy are broad based and relatively well understood, with less distributional consequences than most unconventional balance sheet tools.

Dietch, Peter (2020), 'Legitimacy challenges to central banks: Sketching a way forward', CEP Council of Economic Policies.

ECB (2021), Monetary Policy Decision Minute, December.

English, Bill, Kristin Forbes and Angel Ubide (eds) (2021), *Monetary Policy and Central Banking in the Covid Era: Key Insights and Challenges for the Future.* CEPR Press.

vans, Charles, Jonas Fisher, Francois Gourio and Spencer Krane (2015), 'Risk Management for Monetary Policy Near the Zero Lower Bound', *Brookings Papers on Economic Activity*, 46, 141–219.

Financial Times (2021), 'Quitting QE may be harder than the Bank of England believes', August.

Martinez-Garcia, Enrique. and Rachel Doehr (2022), 'Interest rate expectations shape the Federal Reserve's path of lift-off', Vox, March.

OECD (2021), 'Government at a glance', OECD, Paris. https://doi.org/10.1787/1c258f55-en.

Saunders, Michael (2018), 'Why raise rates? Why limited and gradual?' Bank of England, Speech, April.

Tucker, Paul (2018), *Unelected Power: The Quest for Legitimacy in Central Banking and the Regulatory State*, Princeton University Press.

Vlieghe, Gertjan (2021), 'Running out of room: Revisiting the 3D perspective on low interest rates', Bank of England, Speech.

9 Finding New Objectives, Seeking New Instruments

David Cobham [1]

The adoption of inflation targets in the UK, with the Monetary Policy Committee (MPC) of the Bank given instrument independence in 1997, is often presented as the answer to the assignment problem: the MPC was made responsible for the single objective of price stability, to be attained via its deployment of its single instrument, the policy rate (Allsopp, 2010). In this short chapter I use this perspective to examine the evolution of the workings of monetary policy and the MPC over its first twenty-five years. I outline how the Bank and the MPC came across additional possible objectives and searched for additional possible instruments. I then argue the need for some recasting of the role of the MPC and the way in which it operates.

The Great Moderation, 1997–2007: New Objectives?

The first decade of the MPC is generally seen as highly successful: inflation was kept close to target, and there were fluctuations in output but no recessions. Performance relative to target was enormously better than that in the UK under monetary targets, between the mid-1970s and the mid-1980s, and that under exchange rate targets at different times (including 1991–92).[2] In addition the Bank upgraded its technical expertise, notably in forecasting, improved its communication and came to be recognised internationally as an exemplar of inflation targeting. The arrangements for external members of the MPC were generally satisfactory: there were only occasional tensions about appointments, and the issue of

---

[1] I am grateful to Shane Bonetti and Alex Cobham for helpful comments on an earlier draft.
[2] The classification of monetary policy frameworks at monetaryframeworks.org classifies the UK over the monetary targeting period as 'loosely structured discretion' because the targets were so often missed and as 'loose exchange rate targeting' over 1991–92 because of the wide margins that were maintained until September 1992. On the other hand, the UK is categorised as 'loose inflation targeting' from 1993 to 1996 and as 'full inflation targeting' from 1997 to 2017: there were some overshoots and undershoots, but they were short term, and inflation expectations remained anchored.

Table 9.1 *Inflation, growth and policy rates, averages of quarterly data.*

	1	2	3	4
	1999–2007 mean	1999–2007 standard deviation	2008–2021 mean	2008–2021 standard deviation
Inflation				
UK CPI	1.74	0.48	2.12	1.04
UK HICP*	1.56	0.57	2.26	1.25
Euro Area HICP	2.06	0.43	1.42	1.12
US CPI	2.71	0.76	1.94	1.48
GDP growth				
UK	2.63	0.74	1.06	5.14
Euro Area	2.30	1.12	0.65	3.57
US	2.94	1.30	1.61	2.75
Nominal policy rate				
BoE	4.81	0.74	0.76	1.11
ECB	3.01	0.88	0.62	1.01
Fed	3.60	1.85	0.62	0.78
Real policy rate**				
BoE	3.07	0.85	−1.36	1.21
ECB	0.96	0.90	−0.80	1.01
Fed	0.89	1.64	−1.32	1.46
Nominal shadow policy rate***				
BoE	4.82	0.87	−0.58	2.32
ECB	2.98	0.94	−1.78	2.82
Fed	3.42	2.00	−0.76	2.21
Real shadow policy rate				
BoE	3.08	0.95	−2.77	2.49
ECB	0.93	0.97	−3.22	2.36
Fed	0.71	1.78	−2.53	2.44

Notes: * HICP data to 2020 Q3 only; **ex post, using CPI rates; ***shadow rates to 2019 Q3 only.
Sources: shadow rates from Leo Krippner at www.rbnz.govt.nz/hub/research/additional-re search/measures-of-the-stance-of-us-and-international-monetary-policy (accessed 20.6.22), all other data from International Financial Statistics database (IMF).

external members' access to research assistance was addressed. In terms of international comparisons, the UK looks good (Table 9.1, columns 1 and 2) with lower inflation on average than the Euro Area (in HICP terms) and the US (in CPI terms) and growth which was higher than in the Euro Area though lower than in the US but was more stable.[3]

However, the international comparisons also reveal something rather odd.[4] With inflation on average lower by 0.5% than in the Euro Area and lower by 1% than in the US, the Bank kept its nominal policy rate on average 1.8% higher than the ECB and 1.2% higher than the Federal Reserve. That in turn meant that the real policy rate in the UK was more than 2% higher than in either of the other currency areas. Given the lack of capital controls and the high degree of financial liberalisation, it is difficult to believe that real equilibrium interest rates differed to that extent. A perspective from interest parity relationships would imply that over that period there was a continued expectation of sterling depreciation and/or a significant risk premium attached to the holding of sterling.

As it happens there is considerable evidence of sterling overvaluation throughout the period. Figure 9.1 shows that sterling appreciated sharply in real terms from 1996 and remained well above its 1990–92 level (which is sometimes thought to have been overvalued) until it depreciated sharply from mid-2007. The MPC spent a lot of time discussing this issue in its early years and considered (but never implemented) foreign exchange intervention on several occasions.[5] The IMF was aware of the strong and sustained appreciation but seemed reluctant to identify sterling as overvalued until the sharp correction from mid-2007. However, it then said that, following depreciation of some 25% between mid-2007 and early 2009, 'the currency appears to be broadly in line with fundamentals'.[6] Estimates of the pound's divergence from its fundamental equilibrium (FEER) also suggested significant overvaluation from 1997, particularly against the euro (Wren-Lewis, 2003).

A second issue that arose in the Great Moderation period was that of house prices, which experienced repeated surges with peaks in January 2000, October 2002, June 2004 and July 2007. In the first three cases the MPC was well aware of these developments, to which particular attention was paid by Stephen Nickell who argued that the rises in house prices were essentially the result of structural factors to which the MPC should not respond (Nickell, 2002, 2005). But after he left the MPC in 2006 there was less interest in the issue (Cobham, 2013a).

[3] Obviously, growth rates reflect a range of other factors, so the volatility finding is more important here.
[4] This point was first made in Cobham (2013b).
[5] See Cobham, 2006, for a detailed discussion of the MPC Minutes covering the period.
[6] IMF Article IV Staff Report October 2010 p. 14; see also the reports for February 2005 p. 11, February 2006 p. 11 and February 2007 p. 11.

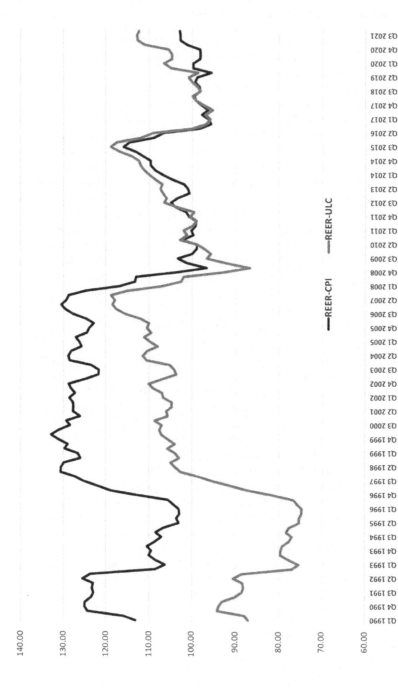

Figure 9.1 Real exchange rates.
Source: International Financial Statistics, accessed 22 June 2022. The REER-CPI is the real effective exchange rate in terms of relative consumer prices; the REER-ULC is the real effective rate in terms of relative unit labour costs.

In principle the MPC could have responded to deviations of both exchange rates and house prices by changing its policy rate, as proposed by Cecchetti et al. (2000) and Cecchetti, Genberg and Wadhwani (2002). Sushil Wadhwani was a member of the MPC from 1999 to 2002 and raised the matter there but never received much support on this: the view of a large majority was always in line with that of Bernanke and Gertler (1999, 2001), which emphasised both the difficulty of identifying asset price bubbles and the possible cost to the real economy of interest rate rises designed to control asset price bubbles (see also Allsopp, 2002; Bean, 2003). With respect to the exchange rate, the MPC considered foreign exchange intervention on several occasions; for example in the August 1997 Minutes (paragraph 61) it was regarded as one of three 'alternative policy instruments that might help to resolve the dilemma without introducing unacceptable distortions' (the others being reserve requirements and changes in debt management), but no such intervention was carried out.

The Global Financial Crisis and Its Aftermath: Objectives and Instruments

In the Great Moderation period the ongoing development of inflation targeting meant that the Bank was heavily focused on price stability, with financial stability treated as a secondary concern, and there was also a widespread view that 'the goal of financial stability is attainable by the means of price stability' (Schwartz, 1995, p. 22). When the GFC erupted in 2007–08, the Bank found itself obliged to adjust its focus and provide liquidity support in various forms to financial institutions which had suddenly become fragile. But it also rapidly became clear that the crisis had profound implications for output and employment, well beyond the kind of short-term cyclical fluctuations assumed in the standard theory of inflation targeting, and that cutting the policy rate in the usual way was not going to be enough.

In early 2009 the Bank initiated quantitative easing (QE), in line with the large-scale asset purchases (LSAPs) introduced by the Fed. At the time this was expected to be a short-term emergency measure, and it was presented as a way of attaining the inflation target when the policy rate was at the effective lower bound. By the end of 2021, however, there had been two rounds of QE in response to the GFC, another designed to steady the economy in the aftermath of the Brexit referendum result in 2016 and three further rounds in response to the Covid-19 pandemic in 2020–21. So QE had become a standard part of the central bank toolbox (see, for example, Friedman, 2015; Bailey et al., 2020).

The first two and the last three rounds were at a time when there were sharp increases in the budget deficit: the government was issuing debt to cover its deficit on the primary market and the Bank was then buying that debt on the secondary market (which meant that it did not violate one of the standard criteria of central bank independence, that the central bank should not intervene in the primary government debt market). In both cases, however, the increases in government debt and the amounts of assets purchased by the Bank were broadly comparable, so that the overall operations looked very much like central bank financing of budget deficits.[7] Given that QE had to be agreed by the Chancellor of the Exchequer (Minister of Finance), these operations also suggested a coordination of fiscal and monetary policy which had not been needed and had not occurred in the Great Moderation period, together with some infringement on the de facto independence of the Bank.

While early QE can be regarded as an appropriate monetary response to an acute downturn when fiscal policy could not react as fast or as strongly, under the coalition government from 2010 with its commitment to fiscal consolidation (austerity) QE became the alternative or substitute to fiscal stimulus.[8] However, the UK economic recovery was slow and weak, and attention turned towards other means to boost activity. There was some discussion of alternatives to inflation targeting, but this did not go far, not least because a change in target – for example, to nominal GDP or its growth rate – might pressure the monetary authorities to do more but would not in itself provide any new instrument (Goodhart et al., 2013; Goodhart, 2015). There was a Funding for Lending Scheme from 2012 and a Help to Buy Scheme from 2013, both joint Bank-Treasury arrangements, designed to subsidise and so encourage banks' lending in the first case and borrowing for house purchase in the second case. While they may have contributed to rises in house prices and to some small increases in lending, Figure 9.2, which shows the principal components of broad money growth, makes clear that bank lending to the private sector

---

[7] See Cobham (2012, p. 738) for 2009–12. For 2020 and 2021 general government gross debt rose by £492 billion between end of 2019 and end of 2021 – see www.ons.gov.uk/economy/governmentpublicsectorandtaxes/publicspending/bulletins/ukgovernmentdebt anddeficitforeurostatmaast/december2021 – while Bank purchases of bonds amounted to £455 billion – see www.bankofengland.co.uk/monetary-policy/quantitative-easing – both accessed 20 June 2022.

[8] Insofar as there was a theoretical (as opposed to political) underpinning to fiscal consolidation in the UK it lay in the ideas of expansionary fiscal contractions and the alleged debt threshold for growth. Those ideas have been comprehensively rebutted, notably by Jordà and Taylor (2013) and Chudik et al. (2017). On the other hand, studies of the effects of QE have typically paid no attention to the accompanying fiscal developments, which could be regarded as providing an additional transmission mechanism for QE.

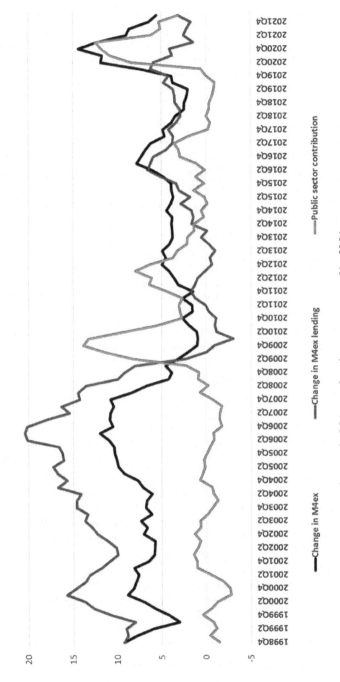

Figure 9.2 Four-quarter changes in M4ex and main counterparts, % of M4ex.
Source: Bank of England statistical database, accessed 22 June 2022.

Change in M4ex — Change in M4ex lending — Public sector contribution

(M4ex)[9] has still not recovered since the GFC to anything like its mid-2000s level.

The next major innovation was forward guidance. This is discussed elsewhere in this volume, but three points are worth making here. First, forward guidance was (thought to be) required only because of the slowness of the economic recovery (related to fiscal consolidation) and the lack of other efficient ways to boost lending and activity. Second, it seems clear that the pressure for forward guidance came from the political authorities (it is also likely that Mark Carney's previous introduction of it at the Bank of Canada was an important factor in his appointment as Governor of the Bank of England) in a further infringement of the Bank's de facto independence. However, it seems that there was then some pushback from the MPC on the details of the scheme and that the pushback made the scheme more complicated, less transparent and, probably, less effective (Cobham, 2013c).

The third, and here most important, point is that the introduction of forward guidance involved a greater emphasis on the short-term trade-off between the attainment of the inflation target and the stabilisation of GDP. The Stockton review (2012, p. 51) had suggested that the Bank's staff should produce for the MPC 'material on alternative possible sequences of actions and their implications for the economic outlook. The material might include information on so-called "optimal" policies and on a variety of alternative rules'. The 2013 Remit for the MPC (Chancellor of the Exchequer, 2013, pp. 3–4) said that the MPC should 'promote understanding of the trade-offs inherent in setting monetary policy to meet a forward-looking inflation target while giving due consideration to output volatility' and that it should set out 'the trade-off that has been made with regard to inflation and output variability in determining the scale and duration of any expected deviation of inflation from the target'. In response Bank staff began to produce, on a regular basis by 2016, what came to be called optimal policy projections, which would allow the MPC to consider the impact on output of different paths for interest rates and inflation. The discussion of this issue was always cast in terms of the primacy of the goal of price stability, but it clearly involved the introduction of a more explicit secondary goal of output stability than had been identified before.

Meanwhile, with regard to asset prices, the Bank, like many other central banks, embraced the possibilities of macroprudential policies,

[9] M4ex (technically M4 excluding intermediate other financial corporations) is the Bank of England's preferred measure of broad money in the UK, so this is the related change in bank lending. The 'public sector contribution' is essentially the amount of monetary financing of the government, including the effect of QE.

which would act more directly on banks' lending to particular sectors such as property. The Financial Policy Committee (FPC), a junior sibling of the MPC, has made use of the countercyclical capital buffer (additional cyclically varying capital requirements for banks) and of two mortgage market measures (a limit on the number of mortgages at high loan-to-income ratios and an affordability test for new borrowers). At the same time the Bank has remained opposed to any monetary leaning against the wind. Indeed, Bean et al. (2010), a paper presented at the 2010 Jackson Hole conference which parallels Bernanke's (2010) paper, argued that in the UK low policy rates in the run-up to the GFC had made only a modest contribution to the rises in credit growth and in house prices and reiterated the view that leaning against the wind, as interpreted in the paper, would have had severe consequences for output.[10]

What do the international comparisons look like for this period? Columns 3 and 4 of Table 9.1 provide comparable data for the period from 2008. First, inflation is now higher than in the Euro Area or the US, while output growth (all currency areas have lower growth than in the Great Moderation period) is intermediate but more volatile. Second, the UK nominal policy rate is marginally higher, but its real policy rate is at the low end, while the UK nominal shadow policy rate and the UK real shadow policy rate are both intermediate: the odd puzzle of the Great Moderation period has disappeared and the real exchange rate (Figure 9.1) is also much lower on average (though the REER-ULC, but not the REER-CPI, rises close to its previous peak in 2015 and again in 2021). This disappearance may, of course, reflect the overall weakness of the UK economy, resulting from austerity and Brexit, rather than any improvement in policymaking.

Assessment

The MPC started out with a clear strategy of pursuing the single objective of price stability with the single instrument of its policy rate. However, over its first twenty-five years the MPC has found itself having to think about other possible objectives – particularly asset prices in the form of exchange rates and house prices, financial stability and output volatility – and adopting other instruments – notably QE and macroprudential policy (wielded by the FPC but with some coordination with the MPC). The question that arises, therefore, is whether it is time to move explicitly on

---

[10] See Cobham (2013a, pp. i59–i60) for the argument that the Bean et al. (2010) model and the Dokko et al. (2009) model on which Bernanke draws both mis-specify expectations and are vulnerable to the Lucas Critique.

from inflation targeting towards a strategy in which, while price stability remains the primary goal, other goals are also admittedly present.

Orphanides (2010, p. 14) wrote that 'inflation targeting may be particularly effective as a monetary policy framework for central banks that are institutionally challenged in some way, for instance because they lack a history of political independence or because they have an impaired credibility in pursuing monetary-stability-oriented policies'. It is arguable that back in 1992–93 with the cataclysmic exit from the Exchange Rate Mechanism the UK really needed the simplicities of inflation targeting to change the perception as well as the direction of monetary policy.[11] But twenty-five years after the Bank acquired basic instrument independence in 1997, with large positive effects on its credibility (Chadha, Macmillan and Nolan, 2007), followed by a long period of relative price stability despite the shocks of the GFC, there is little or no such need.

There is now strong evidence that the adoption of inflation targeting does not in itself necessarily deliver improvements in inflation performance (Ball, 2010; Cobham and Song, 2021). Monetary policy frameworks such as inflation targeting are frameworks for policymaking and they do not dictate individual policy decisions, so that the same decisions can be taken by policymakers from within different frameworks or, indeed, different decisions can be taken by policymakers from within the same framework (Cobham et al., 2022).

It is therefore not clear that anything would be lost by a switch away from simple inflation targeting. On the contrary, a lot could be gained by explicitly adopting a broader set of goals reflecting the shocks to which economies are exposed but retaining the primacy of price stability, perhaps under the tagline of 'inflation targeting plus'. This would recognise the inherently 'messy' nature of central banking (Posen, 2019). At the same time, it would also allow, indeed require, more transparency about the Bank's inevitably circumscribed de facto independence, on the one hand, and about the coordination of fiscal and monetary policy, on the other.

References

Allsopp, Chris (2002), 'Macroeconomic policy rules in theory and in practice', www.bankofengland.co.uk/speech/2002/macroeconomic-policy-rules-in-the ory-and-in-practice (accessed 22 June 2022).

[11] There may be a parallel here with the introduction of monetary targets in the 1970s, which were repeatedly missed but fundamentally changed public perceptions of the nature and role of monetary policy. See Fforde (1983).

Allsopp, Chris (2010), 'Inflation targeting and asset prices', in David Cobham, Oyvind Eitrheim, Stefan Gerlach and Jan Qvigstad (eds.), *Twenty Years of Inflation Targeting: Lessons Learned and Future Prospects*, Cambridge University Press, 172–91.

Bailey, Andrew, Jonathan Bridges, Richard Harrison, Josh Jones and Arkash Mankodi (2020), 'The central bank balance sheet as a policy tool: Past, present and future', Bank of England Staff Working Paper no. 899.

Ball, Laurence (2010), 'The performance of alternative monetary regimes', in Ben Friedman and Michael Woodford (eds.), *Handbook of Monetary Economics*, Volume 3B, 303–43. North Holland.

Bean, Charles (2003), 'Asset prices, financial imbalances and monetary policy: Are inflation targets enough?' Bank for International Settlements Working Paper no. 140.

Bean, Charles, Matthias Paustian, Adrian Penalver and Tim Taylor (2010), 'Monetary policy after the fall', Proceedings – Economic Policy Symposium – Jackson Hole, Federal Reserve Bank of Kansas City, 267–328.

Bernanke, Ben (2010), 'Monetary policy and the housing bubble', www.federalre serve.gov/newsevents/speech/bernanke20100103a.htm (accessed 22 June 2022).

Bernanke, Ben and Mark Gertler (1999), 'Monetary policy and asset price volatility', in 'New challenges for monetary policy', Proceedings – Economic Policy Symposium – Jackson Hole, Federal Reserve Bank of Kansas City, 77–128.

Bernanke, Ben and Mark Gertler (2001), 'Should central banks respond to movements in asset prices?' *American Economic Review*. 91(2), 253–57.

Cecchetti, Stephen, Hans Genberg and Sushil Wadhwani (2002), 'Asset prices in a flexible inflation targeting framework', NBER Working Paper no. 8,970.

Cecchetti, Stephen Hans Genberg, John Lipsky and Sushil Wadhwani (2000), *Asset Prices and Central Bank Policy: Geneva Report on the World Economy no. 2*. Centre for Economic Policy Research.

Chadha, Jagjit, Peter Macmillan and Charles Nolan (2007), 'Independence day for the "Old Lady": A natural experiment on the implications of central bank independence', *Manchester School*. 75(3), 311–27.

Chancellor of the Exchequer (2013), 'Remit for the Monetary Policy Committee', www.bankofengland.co.uk/letter/2013/mpc-remit-march-2013, (accessed 22 June 2022).

Chudik, Alexander, Kammiar Mohaddes, Hashem Pesaran and Mehda Raissi (2017), 'Is there a debt-threshold effect on output growth?' *Review of Economics and Statistics*. 99(1), 135–50.

Cobham, David (2006), 'The overvaluation of sterling since 1996: How the policymakers responded and why', *Economic Journal*. 116 (June), F185–F207.

Cobham, David (2012), 'The past, present and future of central banking', *Oxford Review of Economic Policy*. 28(4), 729–49.

Cobham, David (2013a), 'Central banks and house prices in the run-up to the crisis', *Oxford Economic Papers*. 65(S1), i42–i65.

Cobham, David (2013b), 'Monetary policy under the Labour government 1997–2010: The first 13 years of the MPC', *Oxford Review of Economic Policy*. 29(1), 47–70.

Cobham, David (2013c), 'Forward guidance in the UK: Holding rates down till something happens', in W. den Haan (ed.), *Forward Guidance*, VoxEU ebook.

Cobham, David and Mengdi Song (2021), 'Transitions between monetary policy frameworks and their effects on economic performance', *Economic Modelling*, 95, 311–29.

Cobham, David, Peter Macmillan, Connor Mason and Mengdi Song (2022), 'Economic performance under different monetary policy frameworks', *Journal of Policy Modeling*. 44(2), 431–49.

Dokko, Jane, Brian Doyle, Michael Kiley, Jinil Kim, Shane Sherland, Jae Sim and Skander van der Heuvel. (2009), 'Monetary policy and the housing bubble', Finance and Economics Discussion Paper no. 2009–49, Federal Reserve Board of Governors, Washington, DC.

Fforde, John (1983), 'Setting monetary objectives', *Bank of England Quarterly Bulletin*. 23(2), 200–8.

Friedman, Ben (2015), 'Has the financial crisis permanently changed the practice of monetary policy? Has it changed the theory of monetary policy?' *Manchester School*. 83(S1), 5–19.

Goodhart, Charles (2015), 'Why has monetary policy been comparatively ineffective?' *Manchester School*. 83(S1), 20–9.

Goodhart, Charles, Melanie Baker, Jonathan Ashworth and Anthony O'Brien (2013). 'Monetary targetry: Possible changes under Carney', Morgan Stanley Research Europe.

Jordà, Oscar and Alan Taylor (2013), 'The time for austerity: Estimating the average treatment effect of fiscal policy', *Economic Journal*. 126, 219–55.

Nickell, Stephen (2002), 'House prices, household debt and monetary policy', www.bankofengland.co.uk/speech/2002/house-prices-household-debt-and-monetary-policy (accessed 22 June 2022).

Nickell, Stephen (2005), 'Practical issues in UK monetary policy, 2000–2005', www.bankofengland.co.uk/speech/2005/practical-issues-in-uk-monetary-pol icy-2000-2005 (accessed 22 June 2022).

Orphanides Athanasios (2010), 'Reflections on inflation targeting', in David Cobham, Oyvind Eitrheim, Stefan Gerlach and Jan Qvigstad (eds), *Twenty Years of Inflation Targeting: Lessons Learned and Future Prospects*, Cambridge University Press, 13–24.

Posen, Adam (2019), 'The eroded foundations of inflation targeting', *Manchester School*. 87, (S1), 45–61.

Schwartz, Anna (1995), 'Why financial stability depends on price stability', *Economic Affairs*. 15(4), 21–5.

Stockton, David (2012), 'Review of the Monetary Policy Committee's forecasting capability', www.bankofengland.co.uk/-/media/boe/files/news/2012/novem ber/the-mpcs-forecasting-capability.pdf (accessed 22 June 2022).

Wren-Lewis, Simon (2003), *Estimates of Equilibrium Exchange Rates for Sterling against the Euro*. HM Treasury.

10 Government Debt Management and Monetary Policy Before and After the MPC

William A Allen[1]

Introduction

This chapter describes how the relationship between government debt management and monetary policy has evolved since the late twentieth century. When the Bank's Monetary Policy Committee (MPC) was established in 1997, the relationship was distant, but after the Global Financial Crisis (GFC), with the advent of quantitative easing (QE), the relationship became a very close one, in which debt management objectives were subordinated to monetary policy.

Pre-MPC: Debt Management as Part of Monetary Policy

The Bank was established in 1694 to raise funds for the government. Thus, from its earliest days it was involved in government debt management.

After World War II, in 1946, the ratio of government debt to GDP was 237%. By any standards, the debt was unsustainable and extensive controls over financial transactions were maintained for many years thereafter. Government debt came in several forms:

- Treasury bills, normally of three months' maturity, which were sold at weekly tenders and at other times 'on tap' or ad hoc.
- Gilt-edged securities, or bonds, whose maturity on issue was at least a year but might extend to any number of years: some gilts had no final redemption date.
- Non-marketable savings instruments, aimed at individual investors; and other non-marketable instruments such as certificates of tax deposit.

[1] This chapter owes a great deal to the discussion at the MMF/NIESR symposium on 'The MPC at 25' held on 30 March 2022. It has also benefited greatly from separate discussions with Jagjit Chadha, Richhild Moessner, the late Philip Turner, Anna Watson and Tim Young.

Treasury bills were regarded as liquid assets by the commercial banks and were treated as such for the purposes of the minimum liquidity ratio that, until 1981, the banks were expected to observe. They were traded in the money market, in which the London discount houses were the market-makers. Gilts, in contrast, were not regarded as liquid assets by commercial banks. They were traded in the London Stock Exchange, where the market-makers were jobbing firms, which were unlimited-liability partnerships. After World War II, there were large maturities nearly every year and it was regarded as essential to ensure that there was a market capable of refinancing the maturities and of financing any budget deficit. In the era of high inflation, when money supply targets were used as a means of subduing inflation, gilt sales were used as an instrument for controlling money supply.

The government's need for bond finance has continued and grown in the UK, as it has done in other countries. During the four and a half decades after World War II, inflation was volatile and sometimes very high, and gilt yields were likewise sometimes very high. As noted above, the jobbers in the London Stock Exchange made the market in gilts, but the Bank had become concerned early in World War II that they did not have the capital necessary to handle the turnover associated with the rapidly increasing value of gilts outstanding and sought to supplement the liquidity of the market. In the early 1950s, the Bank began providing liquidity itself, by buying gilts when the prices were falling and selling when they were rising. The functions of market-makers are to facilitate trading by quoting bid and offer prices and to achieve price discovery by matching bids and offers over time. The Bank thus took part in the price discovery process and was led into conflicts between its market-making function and its monetary policy function, which became acute in the 1960s. They were largely resolved in 1971 when, as part of the Competition and Credit Control programme, the scale of the Bank's operations was curtailed. But even after 1971, the jobbers lacked capital resources and could not underwrite tenders for new issues and warehouse gilts until market demand emerged; tenders of new gilt issues continued to be underwritten by the Bank. And the liquidity of the secondary market was supported by a safety net arrangement, under which the Bank would buy a predetermined amount of gilts from them if prices fell by more than a threshold amount that day.[2]

Because gilt sales were so important to monetary policy, it was a matter of acute concern if demand for gilts dried up. Gilt sales were an important influence on decisions about short-term interest rates. Sometimes the

---

[2] Allen (2019, ch 12).

'Grand Old Duke of York' strategy was employed.[3] Short-term interest rates were increased sharply (marched them up to the top of the hill), so as to restore the market's belief that monetary policy was credible and to reduce inflationary expectations; it would then be possible to restart gilt sales, albeit at higher yields than hitherto, and to reduce short-term interest rates gradually (marched them down again).

The need for a safety net for the market-makers was swept away by the 'Big Bang' in the Stock Exchange of 1986, which liberalised the rules of the exchange and enabled the entry into the gilt-edged market of well-capitalised broker-dealers and investment banks as market-makers. The gilt-edged market, having suffered for many years from a chronic dearth of capital, suddenly had a surfeit. Concerns about market liquidity were banished. Moreover, by the mid-1990s, inflation was being subdued and uncertainty about future inflation became a much less potent influence on gilt yields. And after exchange controls were ended in 1979, the gilt market became much more closely integrated with overseas government bond markets.

The need for the Bank to assist in market-making and price discovery diminished, and it became possible to sell gilts by auctions without any need for the Bank to act as an underwriter. A Treasury/Bank review conducted in 1995 concluded that the monetary policy implications of government debt management were now unimportant and a Bank conference held in 1998 reached much the same conclusion.[4] The Treasury saw an opportunity to remove the debt management function from the Bank, when it allowed the Bank autonomy in short-term interest rate management in 1997, and took it. Since 1998, government debt management has been conducted by the Debt Management Office (DMO), an executive agency of the Treasury.

Post-MPC but Pre-Financial Crisis: Debt Management Separate from Monetary Policy

In the DMO's first decade, there was little need for any co-ordination between the DMO and the Bank.[5] The conclusions reached by the Treasury/Bank review of 1995 and by the Bank of England conference

---

[3] Oh, the Grand Old Duke of York,
   He had ten thousand men,
   He marched them up to the top of the hill,
   And he marched them down again.
[4] Her Majesty's Treasury and Bank of England (1995), Chrystal, Haldane and Proudman (1998).
[5] Several Bank of England staff members joined the DMO.

of 1998 proved resilient. Debt management proceeded smoothly, in that market liquidity was ample, auctions of gilts were all or nearly all covered and that there were no serious market disturbances. The Bank of England used information about gilt yields as an indicator of market sentiment but had no voice in to debt management policy, just as the DMO had no voice in to short-term interest rate policy.

Post-Financial Crisis: Debt Management Subordinate to Monetary Policy

The financial crisis of 2008 took central banks and governments by surprise. After the failure of Lehman Brothers in September 2008 and the market disorder that followed, which included abrupt withdrawal of bank credit to non-financial customers, central banks realised that they needed to ease policy quickly.

In the UK, Bank Rate fell from 5% in October 2008 to ½% in March 2009. The MPC wanted to ease further in March 2009 but feared that ½% was the lowest Bank Rate level that it could sustain without damaging the banking system and impairing the functioning of money markets.[6] The MPC then considered the option of QE as an alternative to another Bank Rate cut. This option had been 'pre-cooked': it had been negotiated before the meeting between the Bank and the Treasury. The Chancellor announced the scheme to Parliament on 19 January 2009, when he said that it was a scheme for the Bank to buy privately issued securities and that '[t]he Bank of England will ensure that the total amount of money in the economy does not increase'.[7] The statement that the total amount of money would not increase meant that the asset purchases were to be financed by the issue of Treasury bills or by other operations by the DMO. The Treasury agreed to indemnify the Bank against financial losses; equally it was to benefit from profits. The Bank had 'no economic interest' in the Asset Purchase Facility (APF), the company set up to hold the assets purchased in QE.[8] QE operations were to be subject to the Treasury's approval. The APF bought about £1 billion of commercial paper in February–March 2009, financed by the issue of Treasury bills.[9]

The MPC was invited at its February meeting to endorse a modified version of QE and to ask for the Treasury's agreement to introduce it. In

[6] Bank of England (2009b, paragraph 27).
[7] Hansard, vol. 486 part 15, cols 483–6, 19 January 2009.
[8] Bean (2009). The indemnity is described in the Asset Purchase Facility Annual Reports (e.g. Bank of England, 2021).
[9] Source: Bank of England interactive database, variable YWWB98O.

the modified version, government securities were eligible for purchase, as well as privately issued ones, and the assets would be paid for by crediting the reserve balances of the commercial banks.[10] The Chancellor consented to the modifications.[11]

The MPC agreed unanimously at its March meeting to an initial purchase of up to £75 billion of assets on the modified basis. The minutes record, 'The Committee noted that, in so far as purchases of private sector assets fell short of the £75 billion target, the Bank of England would buy gilts to fulfil the overall quantity of purchases.'[12] The use of the word 'noted' implies that this decision was taken not by the MPC but by the Bank executives. In practice, since 2009 nearly all the Bank's bond purchases have been of government securities. It appeared that the executive managers of the Bank preferred government securities to privately issued ones: for example, Deputy Governor Charles Bean was averse to taking credit risk on to the public sector's balance sheet.[13] In the end, QE was to take enormous amounts of interest rate risk onto the public sector's balance sheet.

The effectiveness of the QE programme as conceived by the Bank's executive management, mainly confined to purchases of gilts, depended on the co-operation of the DMO.[14] It would have undermined the objective of QE if the DMO had lengthened the maturity of its own sales. The Chancellor concurred in his letter to the Governor of 3 March 2009 when he wrote 'I recognise the importance of ensuring that debt management policy is consistent with the aims of monetary policy.'[15] This statement, which subordinated debt management to monetary policy, was to have extensive and expensive consequences.

QE had been introduced as an emergency measure, on a moderate scale, in a financial crisis. However, the economy was slow to recover and QE was used again in 2010–12. After the referendum vote to leave the European Union in 2016, it was used yet again. That took the total up to £435 billion (there had been no unwinding).

---

[10] Bank of England (2009a, paragraphs 35–9).

[11] Letter from Chancellor to Governor, 3 March 2009, www.bankofengland.co.uk/letter/2009/apf-letter-march-2009.

[12] Bank of England (2009b, paragraph 45).

[13] Bean (2009). Goodfriend (2011) argues that the Federal Reserve 'should adhere to a 'Treasuries only' asset acquisition policy except for occasional and limited discount window lending to depository institutions deemed to be solvent'.

[14] However, the Bank of England conducted the gilt purchases itself, rather than by using the DMO as a purchasing agent. Breedon and Turner (2016) compute the transaction costs and conclude that the design of the Bank of England's purchasing auctions was inferior to that of the reverse auctions that the DMO had conducted in 2000–01.

[15] Letter from Chancellor to Governor, 3 March 2009, www.bankofengland.co.uk/letter/2009/apf-letter-march-2009.

The first financial manifestation of the coronavirus pandemic was a large global wave of sales of government securities in March 2020, after it had become clear that the pandemic would lead to widespread lockdowns and economic disclocation, and to enlarged budget deficits. In the UK, the gilt-edged market weakened sharply on 18 March when the quoted 20-year yield rose from 1.05% to 1.36% and ceased to function on 19 March after a gilt auction. The DMO feared that it would be unable to sell as many gilts as it needed to without extraordinary support.[16]

The MPC held an emergency meeting that same day. The minutes record that it was convened 'to consider the response of monetary policy to the economic shock from Covid-19', but it is clear from a subsequent interview with the Chief Executive Officer of the DMO in *The Times* that the trigger was the breakdown in the gilt market.[17] The MPC decided on its first quantitative easing operation of 2020: it resolved to buy £200 billion of gilts. Its stated objective was to 'improve the functioning of the gilt market and help to counteract a tightening of monetary and financial conditions that would put at risk the MPC's objectives'.[18] It later characterised the pursuit of the first of these objectives as acting as market-maker of last resort.[19] The initial £200 billion was followed up with another £250 billion. That took the total up to £895 billion (including £20 billion of corporate bonds) and the purchasing programme was completed in December 2021.

There is no reason to believe that any request from the MPC to undertake more quantitative easing has been turned down by the Treasury. Thus, the subordination of debt management to monetary policy in which Chancellor Darling acquiesced in March 2009 was maintained for over a dozen years.

The Maturity of the Government Debt

Whatever the effects of QE on inflation and output may have been, one of its consequences was that the maturity structure of the government's financial liabilities was heavily concentrated at zero maturity: at the end of the programme, the APF had a liability of £895 billion, or 36% of GDP, to the Issue Department of the Bank, for which the Treasury is responsible.[20]

---

[16] Aldrick (2020).   [17] Bank of England (2020a, paragraph 1), Aldrick (2020).
[18] Bank of England (2020a, 2020b). That day, 18 March, was the first day of Andrew Bailey's term of office as governor of the Bank of England. Truly a baptism of fire.
[19] See for example Hauser (2021).
[20] Source: Bank of England Asset Purchase Facility Fund Ltd (2022). Data are as at 28 February 2022.

The liability bears interest at Bank Rate. That means that the public finances are very sensitive to decisions made about Bank Rate by the MPC.

This aspect of QE has been known and understood for a long time (Allen, 2017, 2021; OBR, 2021). Indeed, for several years, the APF produced an unrealised profit, which was remitted to the Treasury and spent. The total amount remitted to the Treasury was £120 billion at the end of February 2022.[21] Now that interest rates have started to rise and gilt prices have fallen, on my calculations the APF has incurred losses much larger than the earlier profits.

There is accordingly a fiscal cost, and an ongoing fiscal risk. An increase in interest rates across the yield curve of just one basis point would reduce the value of the portfolio by £400 million.[22]

Moreover, there is a risk to the MPC.[23] The powerful implications of the MPC's decisions for the public finances and the maintenance of a large balance sheet by the Bank of England both threaten the Bank's independence.[24] There is a heightened risk of fiscal dominance[25] of monetary policy which would undermine the MPC's ability to meet its price stability objective.[26] Finally, as banker to the government, the Bank has an obligation not to act contrary to the government's financial interests.

The fiscal risks and the threat to the Bank's independence are both powerful reasons for unwinding QE promptly. This author and others put forward in 2021 a proposal to reduce quickly the egregious exposure of the public finances to Bank Rate.[27] The MPC, however, displayed no sign of urgency. It said in August 2021 that it would stop reinvesting the redemption proceeds of maturing gilts in its portfolio when Bank Rate reached 0.5%, which occurred in February 2022. However, the portfolio had a very long maturity: at the end of the programme, its half-life was nearly 8 years and its average maturity 13 years.[28] The MPC said that it would consider the possibility of active sales when Bank Rate reached 1%; when that happened in May 2022, it said it would consider beginning active sales and promised an update in August.[29]

---

[21] Busetto, Chavaz, Froemel et al. (2022). Box D of this Bank of England article gives a clear account of the cash flows associated with QE.

[22] My calculation, as at 31st March 2024.

[23] For quantification of the possible effects of the risk, see Office for Budget Responsibility (2021, Chapter 4).

[24] Allen (2017).   [25] Sargent and Wallace (1981).   [26] Sargent and Wallace (1981).

[27] Allen (2021); Allen, Chadha and Turner (2021).

[28] Author's calculation from Bank of England data.   [29] Bank of England (2021, 2022b).

Maintaining a large portfolio of gilts with long average maturity financed by short-term borrowing implies large financial risks for the government and threatens the independence of the Bank. Quantitative tightening has now begun, and lengthening the maturity of the government's debt should remain a matter of high priority.

References

Aldrick, Philip (2020), 'The day the financial world stood still' and 'Bank of England rode to government's rescue as gilt markets froze', interview with Sir Robert Stheeman, *The Times*, 30 April.

Allen, William (2017), 'Quantitative easing and the independence of the Bank of England', *National Institute Economic Review*. 241, R65–R69.

Allen, William (2019), *The Bank of England and the Government Debt: Operations in the Gilt-Edged Market, 1928 – 1972*, Cambridge University Press.

Allen, William (2021), 'Managing the fiscal risk of higher interest rates' NIESR Policy Paper 025, 26 March, www.niesr.ac.uk/publications/managing-fiscal-risk-higher-interest-rates?type=policy-papers.

Allen, William, Jagjit Chadha and Philip Turner (2021), 'Quantitative tightening: Protecting monetary policy from fiscal encroachment', NIESR Policy Paper 27, 28 July, www.niesr.ac.uk/publications/quantitative-tightening-protecting-mon etary-policy-fiscal-encroachment?type=policy-papers.

Bank of England (2009a), Minutes of Monetary Policy Committee meeting, February, www.bankofengland.co.uk/minutes/2009/monetary-policy-commit tee-february-2009.

Bank of England (2009b), Minutes of Monetary Policy Committee meeting, March, www.bankofengland.co.uk/minutes/2009/monetary-policy-commit tee-march-2009.

Bank of England (2020a), 'Minutes of the special Bank of England Monetary Policy Committee meeting on 19th March 2020 and the Monetary Policy Committee meeting ending on 25th March 2020', www.bankofengland.co.uk/ monetary-policy-summary-and-minutes/2020/march-2020.

Bank of England (2020b), 'APF: Additional gilt purchases', 19 March, www.bank ofengland.co.uk/markets/market-notices/2020/apf-asset-purchases-and-tfsme-march-2020.

Bank of England (2021), 'Monetary Policy Report', August, www.bankofeng land.co.uk/monetary-policy-report/2021/august-2021.

Bank of England (2022a), 'Bank of England Asset Purchase Facility Fund Ltd, annual report and accounts, 1st March 2021 – 28th February 2022', www.bank ofengland.co.uk/asset-purchase-facility/2022/2021-22.

Bank of England (2022b), 'Minutes of Monetary Policy Committee meeting, May', www.bankofengland.co.uk/monetary-policy-summary-and-minutes/20 22/may-2022.

Bean, Charles (2009), 'Quantitative easing: An interim report', speech given at the London Society of Chartered Accountants Annual Lunch, London, 13 October, www.bankofengland.co.uk/speech/2009/quantitative-easing-and-interim-report.

Breedon, Francis and Philip Turner (2016), 'On the transactions costs of quantitative easing', BIS Working Paper no. 571, www.bis.org/publ/work571.htm.

Busetto, Filippo, Matthieu Chavaz, Maren Froemel et al. (2022), 'QE at the Bank of England: A perspective on its functioning and effectiveness', Bank of England *Quarterly Bulletin*, Q1, www.bankofengland.co.uk/quarterly-bulletin/2022/2022-q1/qe-at-the-bank-of-england-a-perspective-on-its-functioning-and-effectiveness.

Chrystal, Alec, Andrew Haldane and James Proudman (eds.) (1998), 'Government debt structure and monetary conditions', Bank of England.

Goodfriend, Marvin (2011), 'Central banking in the credit turmoil: An assessment of Federal Reserve practice', *Journal of Monetary Economics*. 58 (1), 1–12.

Hauser, Andrew (2021), 'From lender of last resort to market maker of last resort via the dash for cash: Why central banks need new tools for dealing with market dysfunction', speech at Reuters, London, 7 January, www.bankofengland.co.uk/speech/2021/january/andrew-hauser-speech-at-thomson-reuters-newsmaker.

Her Majesty's Treasury and Bank of England (1995), 'Report of the debt management review, July', www.dmo.gov.uk/documentview.aspx?docname=remit/report95.pdf&page=Remit/fulldetails.

Office for Budget Responsibility (2021), 'Fiscal risks report, London', obr.uk/frr/fiscal-risks-report-july-2021/.

Sargent, Thomas and Neil Wallace (1981), 'Some unpleasant monetarist arithmetic', Federal Reserve Bank of Minneapolis Quarterly Review, Fall.

IV

MPC Process

11   An Analysis of Central Bank Decision-Making

Maria Demertzis, Catarina Martins and Nicola Viegi

Introduction

The way central banks take monetary policy decisions has evolved over the years. One important shift has been the assigning of monetary policy decisions to a committee rather than to one individual. In May 1997, then Chancellor of the Exchequer Gordon Brown granted the Bank of England operational independence, in other words, the independence to decide how to achieve price stability. By contrast, the Bank was not granted target independence; the definition of price stability, the inflation target, remained with the government. Under the Bank of England Act (see Rodgers, 1998), which came into force on 1 June 1998, the Monetary Policy Committee (MPC) decides on the monetary policy measures to achieve the inflation target. The act specified the composition of the MPC as the Bank of England governor, two deputy governors, two members appointed by banks, and four external members appointed by the chancellor.

In the case of the European Central Bank (ECB), its establishment in January 1999 as a centralised body responsible for monetary policy was contemporaneous with the introduction of the euro as an official currency in 11 EU countries. The responsibility for monetary policy was then transferred from each of the central banks of those countries to the ECB. Since then, the number of euro-area countries has expanded to 19. The governors of the euro-area national central banks still have a say in monetary policy decisions since the ECB Governing Council comprises the governors of each national central bank in addition to six members of the ECB executive board.

The Federal Reserve System, created in 1913 with the Federal Reserve Act, started as a system of 12 Reserve Banks operating independently. As the US economy became more integrated, more collaboration and coordination were needed, resulting in convergence on more centralised decision-making. Revisions to the Federal Reserve Act in 1933 and 1935 led to the creation of the Federal Open Market Committee (FOMC), which is still today the Fed's monetary policy decision-making body. The FOMC is composed of the members of the board of governors – nominated by the president of the US and confirmed in their positions by the US Senate – and the Bank Reserve presidents.

In 2022, the Bank of England MPC celebrates 25 years, and we use this occasion to compare its decision-making process to that of the ECB and the Federal Reserve.

What Makes an Effective Decision-Making Process?

Table 11.1 summarises, as of May 2022, some of the core elements of the decision-making process at the Bank of England, the ECB and the Federal Reserve Board. The pursuit of price stability by a committee is by now the standard in central banking.

The move towards committees somewhat coincided with the shift to central bank independence (Blinder, 2007) in the late twentieth century. This was a natural consequence of central banks no longer taking orders from their governments but being given the operational independence to pursue pre-defined economic objectives, generally inflation related. Members of committees then needed to pool the information that would help them make good decisions in uncertain circumstances – a necessary step when performing complex tasks like monetary policy. The move towards central bank independence was crucial to ensure politically independent and goal-oriented conduct of monetary policy. The more long-term orientation and objectivity of monetary policy's goals – contrasting with the shorter-term nature of political cycles and political bias to inflate the economy – proved beneficial to price stability, with more credible signals helping to manage inflation expectations (Bernanke, 2010; Haldane, 2020).

But decision-making by committees is not identical in all central banks (Blinder, 2007). Broadly speaking, central bank committees fall into two categories: individualistic, in which each member expresses his or her own opinion and votes accordingly, and collegial, in which members reach decisions collectively and stand by them. The Bank of England is an example of the former. An individualistic system is built on the diversity of views and aims to reduce the risk of groupthinking. On the other hand, however, when votes are split, they face the challenge of communicating effectively to the public the rationale behind any decision. The ECB, by contrast, has a collegial-based system, in which decisions reached are presented as decisions of the whole decision-making body. The emphasis is on communicating one view and therefore claiming

Table 11.1 *The decision-making process in three main central banks as of May 2022.*

	Bank of England	European Central Bank	Fed
Decision-making			
Decision-making body	Monetary Policy Committee (MPC)	Governing Council	Federal Open Market Committee (FOMC)
Number of members	9	25	12
Composition of the decision-making body	The governor + 3 deputy governors + the chief economist + 4 external members	6 members of the executive board + the governors of the national central banks of the 19 euro-area countries	7 members of the board of governors + the president of the Federal Reserve Bank of New York + 4 of the remaining 11 Reserve Bank presidents (one-year term on a rotating basis)
Gender distribution	7 male + 2 female (both external members)	23 male + 2 female (both in exec board)	5 male + 5 female**
Nationalities	Mixed but mostly British	All euro-area nationalities	US citizens
Who has the right to vote	All 9 members of the MPC	6 exec board members vote permanently + 15 votes from 19 NCB governors (monthly rotating basis*)	The 12 members of the FOMC (yearly rotation for the RB presidents***)
Reaching a decision	Voting	Collegial	Voting
Disclosure of voting	Yes	No	Yes
Frequency of meetings	8 times a year	Every six weeks (~ 8 times a year)	Typically, 8 times a year

Source: Bruegel.
Notes: The composition described is for 2022, not historical.
*ECB rotating voting: since 2015, there are 15 votes gathered from the 19 National Central Bank Governors on a monthly rotating basis. There are two groups of countries: big (4 votes) and small (11 votes). All (6+19) participate in the discussions.
**In view of resignations and no replacement up to this point, the numbers do not add up to the expected 12 FOMC members.
***Note that all 12 Reserve Bank presidents attend FOMC meetings and participate in the discussions.

ownership by all who participate. In the case of the Fed, while the FOMC members vote and those votes are then published, a statement is issued in the name of the FOMC and the final decision is embraced by all members. Hence, it is a collegial type of committee, though different from the ECB.

Many attempts have been made in the literature to identify what makes a committee effective. Having clear objectives, efficient instruments and independence are of prime importance (Maier, 2010). A manageable size, not much larger than five members, is also viewed as preferable (Hansen, McMahon and Rivera, 2014). However, restricting the size is not always possible. Berger, Nitsch and Lybek (2008) looked at a sample of 84 central banks around the world and verified that the size of decision-making bodies was around seven to nine members. It seems that MPC size increases with country size, population heterogeneity and with democratic political regimes. In cases where committees have a large number of members, a rotation system may help combine a manageable size with bringing in more information (Maier, 2010). However, as it becomes harder to evaluate the effort put into individual contributions in larger committees, members may feel tempted to free-ride or shirk and end-up contributing less to the pooling of information. A system that identifies members' contributions may help reduce this risk, leading to higher quality of contributions and resulting in more effective information collection to better inform monetary policy decisions. The diversity of members' backgrounds, for example in the form of internal and external members, also adds to the information set and can help avoid extreme ideas or groupthinking.

Linked to the two types of committee decision-making is the role of statements and minutes as part of the communication process. Individualistic committees use minutes a lot more as a way of communicating both decisions reached and points of disagreement. Detailed statements, on the other hand, are a more effective tool in collegial central banks. As Paul Tucker, a former BoE MPC member, puts it, this is because 'it is more difficult for us than for some of our peers to release an informative statement immediately after the policy meeting: if you don't know what you're going to decide, it is pretty hard to prepare a draft in advance!' (Tucker, 2008).

A number of studies have examined how the characteristics of members of monetary policy committees affect decision-making. The literature that investigates the Fed's FOMC looks at educational and career characteristics and differences in behaviour between political appointees (such as the Governor who is appointed by the US president) and bank presidents. Eichler, Lahner and Noth (2018) found that FOMC members who have a financial industry background or represent a region with a large banking sector are more sensitive to local banking instability. Smales and Apergis (2016) found that the tenure of the FOMC chair and their experience in government lead to more dovish decisions. Hansen and McMahon (2016) reach a similar conclusion regarding governor tenure for the MPC. Signalling a tougher stance at the beginning of the tenure leads to a better anchoring of future inflation expectations. By contrast, the longer the period as bank staff, the greater the tendency for hawkish decisions, since there is a greater preference for lower levels of inflation aligned with price level stability. Internal disagreements are very much attributed to the background characteristics of FOMC members and to political influence (Bennani, Kranz and Neuenkirch, 2018).

Authors who study the workings of the Bank of England's MPC have also analysed the relevance and importance of dissent. Given the set-up of the MPC, many have studied how the distinction between internal and external members plays out. Harris, Levine and Spencer (2011) showed that external members are more likely to dissent when the MPC's inflation forecast deviates from the target. Gerlach-Kristen (2009) argued that insiders typically attach greater weight to inflation stabilization than external members, who are more dovish. Gerlach-Kristen (2009) attributed this to the fact that externals are appointed (and potentially reappointed) by the chancellor, which gives them an incentive to be more 'recession averse'. Harris and Spencer (2009) showed that insiders tend to vote as a bloc and are typically on the winning side of policy decisions, given their numeric superiority. Hansen, McMahon and Rivera (2014) also found that internal MPC members have superior expertise compared to externals, which casts some doubt on the value-added of external members. However, Hansen, McMahon and Rivera (2014) and others, particularly Downward and Mearman (2007), pointed to the importance of triangulation or the use of diverse sources of information to inform decisions. Such diverse sources could range from different methods and data to different theories and researchers.

Last, other streams of literature have focused on different aspects including the relevance of nationality, particularly in the context of the ECB, and gender. Badinger and Nitsch (2011) studied the ECB and showed that indeed beyond a certain management level, nationality does affect the formulation of monetary policy. The issue of gender has been subject to growing attention, and an increasing number of studies examine to what extent gender affects monetary policy decisions. Rieder (2022) showed that there is mixed evidence in the literature and advises caution given the current small proportion of women in the samples used to investigate this topic.

Individualistic versus Collegial: Are They Really That Different?

While many attempts have been made to understand what makes an efficient decision-making set-up, much less is known and understood about why central banks might opt for one system or the other.

The reasons often probably have little to do with what is known about optimal design and more to do with culture or broader political economy contexts. Malmendier, Nagel and Yan (2021) showed that differences between FOMC members' inflation expectations and Fed staff forecasts can be explained by personal lifetime experiences of inflation and do affect voting outcomes.

Arguably, this link between preferences and experience is why the ECB opted to pursue a consensus model in its decision-making (Claeys and Linta, 2019). The idea was that if the ECB was to speak for the Euro Area, as indeed dictated by its mandate, then it had to ignore national preferences. And to be able to convince the public, it would have to speak with one voice. The decision-making process and the communication of decisions would therefore not provide any information on disagreements or the extent of consensus. Also, even if the optimal size of a committee is shown to be around five members, for political economy reasons the ECB could not afford to not include all national central banks in its decision-making body.[1]

The question then is whether the set-up of any given committee actually leads to very different ways of deliberating. Ehrmann and Fratzscher (2007) showed that there is not a single best approach for central banks to adopt. Different ways of combining more or less individualistic communication and decision-making strategies may deliver similarly good results in terms of responsiveness of financial markets and predictability of policy decisions. Similarly, Riboni and Ruge-Murcia (2010) looked at five different central banks (Bank of England, ECB, Fed, Bank of Canada and the Swedish Riksbank) and concluded that, despite having different formal committee types, all central banks seem to follow a consensus model in the way they take actual interest-rate decisions. We take a closer look at the way the Bank of England, the Fed and the ECB reach decisions and confirm that, irrespective of the set-up, their approach to consensus building when they make decisions is similar.

Figures 11.1–11.3 plot all rate decisions since the late 1990s taken by the Bank of England, the Fed and the ECB. Also, we report the degree of agreement reached in each decision. Data is available for the Bank of

---

[1] Country participation is the sine-qua-non in any European institution (see Commissioners at the European Commission or members of the ESM).

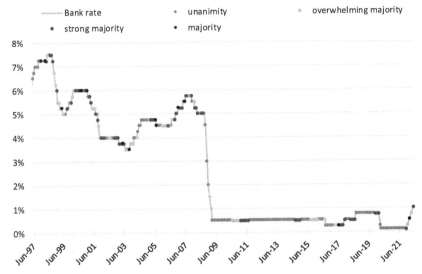

Figure 11.1 BoE MPC voting decisions on the Bank Rate.
Source: Bruegel based on Bank of England. Notes: period from
June 1997 to May 2022. Unanimity = all votes in support;
overwhelming majority = all − 1 vote; strong majority = between
strong majority (all − 1) and majority; majority = half + 1 votes in
support.

England and for the Fed as votes are published after each meeting but not
for the ECB, since it does not publish votes. Hence, we rely on the
methodology of Claeys and Linta (2019), who gathered information
from various sources on how decisions were taken.[2]

We observe that, at the current juncture, the Bank of England faces
greater disagreement – dissent as captured by voting, not by discussions –
than during earlier times.[3] The same feature is not so evident for the Fed
or the ECB. This could be explained by the early action on interest rate
hikes taken by the Bank since the end of 2021 as a response to the surge in
inflation, while the Fed took action to increase its Federal Funds target
range only in March 2022 and the ECB still hasn't taken any action on
that front.

---

[2] These include the transcripts of the press conferences following the Governing Council
'monetary policy' meetings which also include transcripts of the Q&A with journalists and,
since 2015, the 'accounts', that is, the summaries of the discussion of the monetary policy
meetings published by the ECB. Exceptional press releases may also be considered.
[3] This does not mean it is more or less than the ideal amount of dissent which itself could
vary over time.

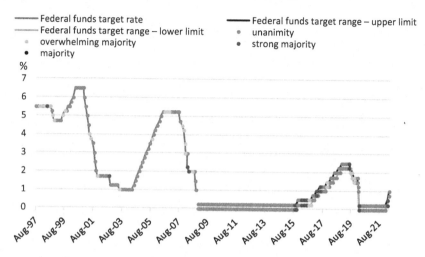

Figure 11.2 Fed FOMC voting decisions on the federal funds target rate/range.
Source: Bruegel based on Federal Reserve. Notes: period from August 1997 to May 2022. Until October 2008, the FOMC defined a target rate for the Federal Funds Rate. From December 2008, the FOMC defined a target range with an upper and lower limit within which the effective Federal Funds rates could fluctuate. Unanimity = all votes in support; overwhelming majority = all − 1 vote; strong majority = between strong majority (all − 1) and majority, majority = half + 1 vote in support.

For nearly two-thirds (61%) of ECB meetings, we have no information on the degree of consensus reached for interest-rate decisions. Figures 11.4–11.6 summarise the degree of disagreement during deliberations of the three central banks, differentiating between decisions on interest rates and asset purchases. Despite the ECB decision-making process relying on consensus, the degree of unanimity reached is quite similar to that of the Bank of England when it comes to interest-rate decisions. Out of the three banks, the Fed reaches rate decisions with unanimity most often (around 80% of the time). This is not surprising given the historically low levels of dissent in the FOMC, even though it fluctuates over time (Thornton and Wheelock, 2014).

When it comes to unconventional measures, in this case asset purchases, the Bank of England and the Fed show similar patterns. The members of these two banks reach unanimity much more frequently than the ECB. That is to be expected because when it comes to asset purchases, the ECB buys a much wider portfolio of bonds with different risks.

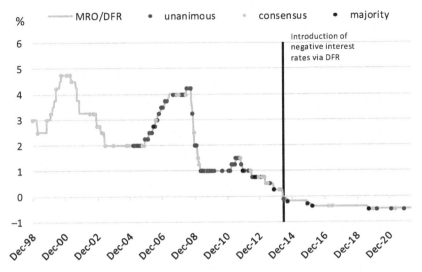

Figure 11.3 ECB Governing Council decisions on the main refinancing rate (MRO) and deposit facility rate (DFR).
Source: Bruegel based on ECB. Notes: period from December 1998 to May 2022. Before 5 June 2014, the rate plotted corresponds to the MRO, after that to the DFR. The classification of the decision was made according to what was indicated by the ECB president in press conferences and by the monetary policy accounts, based on Claeys and Linta (2019).

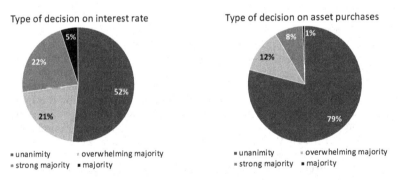

Figure 11.4 BoE MPC Bank Rate and asset purchases decisions.
Notes: period from June 1997 to May 2022. Unanimity = all votes in support; overwhelming majority = all − 1 vote; strong majority = between strong majority (all − 1) and majority; majority = half + 1 votes in support.
Source: Bruegel based on Bank of England.

Type of decision on interest rate/range

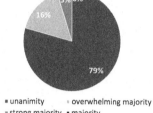

Type of decision on asset purchases

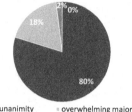

Figure 11.5 Fed FOMC federal funds target and asset purchases decisions.

Notes: period from August 1997 to May 2022. Unanimity = all votes in support; overwhelming majority = all − 1 vote; strong majority = between strong majority (all − 1) and majority, majority = half + 1 votes in support.
Source: Bruegel based on Federal Reserve.

Type of decision on interest rates

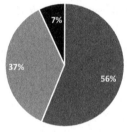

Type of decision on asset purchases

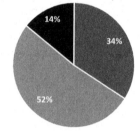

Figure 11.6 ECB Governing Council interest rates and asset purchases decisions.

Notes: period from December 1998 to May 2022. The classification of the decision was made according to what was indicated by the ECB president in the press conferences and by the monetary policy accounts. Note that, for the BoE chart, we show decisions on bond purchases, while for the ECB 'other' includes more policies, for example, forward guidance or credit operations.
Source: Bruegel based on ECB and Claeys and Linta (2019).

We then analyse level of disagreement considering also the direction of the policy move: 'easing' when the policy is meant to stimulate the economy and bring inflation up when it is below target and 'tightening' when the policy acts as a break to economic overheating and aims to reduce inflation that is above target. There is also a third category 'maintain' for the cases in which there in no change in the policy. In the case of rates, a decrease (increase) in rate is classified as easing (tightening). In the case of asset purchases, if the policy implies an increase (decrease) in the size of the balance sheet, it was classified as easing (tightening).

The one characteristic the three central banks share is that they reach tightening interest rate decisions more often by unanimity than easing decisions (Figure 11.7). We can also see that, when it comes to

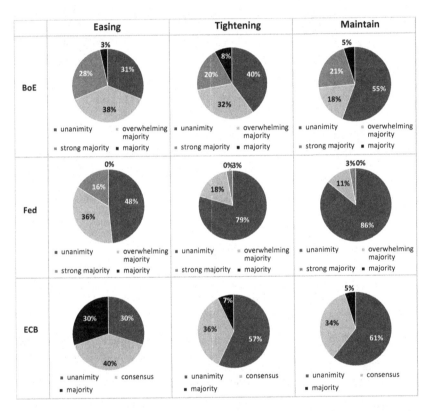

Figure 11.7 Level of disagreement and direction of policy move: for interest rates.
Notes: period from June 1997 to May 2022 for BoE, from August 1997 to May 2022 for Fed, from December 1998 to May 2022 for ECB. For the ECB, the classification of the decision was made according to what was indicated by the ECB president in the press conferences and by the monetary policy accounts.
Source: Bruegel based on BoE, Fed and ECB.

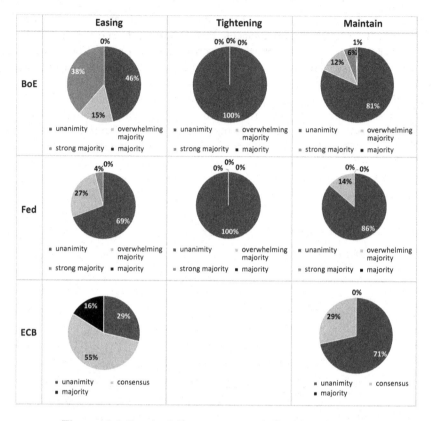

Figure 11.8 Level of disagreement and direction of policy move: for asset purchases.

Notes: period from June 1997 to May 2022 for BoE, from August 1997 to May 2022 for Fed, from December 1998 to May 2022 for ECB. Only decisions with regard to asset purchases were considered. For the ECB, the classification of the decision was made according to what was indicated by the ECB president in the press conferences and by the monetary policy accounts. For the BoE and the Fed, the pies for tightening reflect two decisions each.

Source: Bruegel based on BoE, Fed and ECB.

maintaining the policy unchanged, the decision is backed usually by most members.

Regarding asset purchases, as Figure 11.8 shows, there is a limited historical record on tightening decisions. This is not surprising given that unconventional tools have been only relatively recently deployed by the three central banks. Comparing easing decisions with those on maintaining the size of the balance sheet, we still see more agreement on the latter. The distribution of the levels of agreement is very similar to that on decisions on interest rates.

Conclusions

Central bank monetary policy decisions are generally taken by committees, independently from governments. The formal set-up of these committees varies and so does the way of deliberating. Some vote; others seek consensus. A relevant question is whether the committee type in practice leads to differences in how members reach monetary policy decisions. Based on an analysis of the Bank of England, the Federal Reserve and the ECB, we conclude that the three banks value reaching decisions by unanimity. This result is more pronounced for tightening than for easing decisions; tightening decisions are more often taken by unanimity. This is perhaps not surprising given the impact central bank actions have on the economy. Central banks want to provide clear signals in order to be convincing.

References

Badinger, Harald and Volker Nitsch (2011), 'National representation in multinational institutions: The case of the European Central Bank'. Working Paper No. 3573. CESifo Working Papers.

Bennani, Ham, Tobias Kranz and Matthias Neuenkirch (2018), 'Disagreement between FOMC members and the Fed's staff: New insights based on a counterfactual interest rate', *Journal of Macroeconomics*. 58, 139–53.

Berger, Helge, Volker Nitsch and Tonny Lybek (2008), 'Central bank boards around the world: Why does membership size differ?' *European Journal of Political Economy*. 24(4), 817–32.

Bernanke, Ben S. (2010), 'Central bank independence, transparency, and accountability'. In Institute for Monetary and Economic Studies International Conference. Bank of Japan, Tokyo. www.federalreserve.gov/newsevents/speech/bernanke20100525a.htm.

Blinder, Alan S. (2007), 'Monetary policy by committee: Why and how?' *European Journal of Political Economy*. 23(1), 106–23.

Claeys, Gregory and Tanja Linta (2019), 'The evolution of the ECB governing council's decision-making | Bruegel'. June 2019. www.bruegel.org/2019/06/the-evolution-of-the-ecb-governing-councils-decision-making/.

Downward, Paul and Andrew Mearman (2007), 'Decision-making at the Bank of England: A critical appraisal', *Oxford Economic Papers*. 60(October), 385–409.

Ehrmann, Michael and Marcel Fratzscher (2007), 'Communication by central bank committee members: Different strategies, same effectiveness?' *Journal of Money, Credit and Banking*. 39(2–3), 509–41.

Eichler, Stefan, Tom Lähner and Felix Noth (2018), 'Regional banking instability and FOMC voting', *Journal of Banking and Finance*. 87, 282–92.

Gerlach-Kristen, Petra (2009), 'Outsiders at the Bank of England's MPC', *Journal of Money, Credit and Banking*. 41(6), 1099–115.

Haldane, Andy (2020), 'What has central bank independence ever done for us?' In UCL Economists' Society Economics Conference. www.bankofengland.co.uk/-/media/boe/files/speech/2020/what-has-central-bank-independence-ever-done-for-us-speech-by-andy-haldane.pdf.

Hansen, Stephen, Michael McMahon and Carlos Velasco Rivera (2014), 'Preferences or private assessments on a monetary policy committee?' *Journal of Monetary Economics*. 67, 16–32.

Hansen, Stephen and Michael McMahon (2016), Understanding the macroeconomic effects of central bank communication. *Journal of International Economics*. 99(S1), S114–S133.

Harris, Mark N. and Christopher Spencer (2009), 'The policy choices and reaction functions of Bank of England MPC members', *Southern Economic Journal*. 76(2), 482–99.

Harris, Mark N., Paul Levine and Christopher Spencer (2011), 'A decade of dissent: Explaining the dissent voting behavior of Bank of England MPC members', *Public Choice*. 146(3), 413–42.

Maier, Philipp (2010), 'How central banks take decisions: An analysis of monetary policy meetings', in Pierre L. Siklos, Martin T. Bohl and Mark E. Wohar (eds.), *Challenges in Central Banking*, 320–56. Cambridge University Press.

Malmendier, Ulrike, Stefen Nagel and Zhen Yan (2021), 'The making of hawks and doves'. *Journal of Monetary Economics*. 117, 19–42.

Riboni, Alessandro and Francisco J Ruge-Murcia (2010), 'Monetary policy by committee: Consensus, chairman dominance or simple majority?' *The Quarterly Journal of Economics*. 125(1), 363–416.

Rieder, Kilian (2022), 'Monetary policy decision-making by committee: Why, when and how it can work', *European Journal of Political Economy*. 72(2), 102091.

Rodgers, Peter (1998), 'The Bank of England Act', Quarterly Bulletin, Q2, Bank of England. 93–99.

Smales, Lee A. and Nick Apergis (2016), 'The influence of FOMC member characteristics on the monetary policy decision-making process'. *Journal of Banking & Finance*. 64(March), 216–31.

Thornton, Daniel L. and David C. Wheelock (2014), 'Making sense of dissents: A history of FOMC dissents', *Federal Reserve Bank of St. Louis Review*. 96(3), 213–27.

Tucker, Paul (2008), 'Remarks on "making monetary policy by committee"', *Bank of England Quarterly Bulletin*. 48(3), 347–50.

12 The Decision-Making Process
The 'Groupvote' Phenomenon

Richard Barwell

Introduction

Monetary policy decisions in the UK are made by a committee of nine individuals on a one-member one-vote basis. There is nothing unusual about that. Decision by committee, rather than by individual, has been the norm in central banking (Blinder, 2004) for several decades.

The members of those policy committees don't always vote the same way. The frequency of dissenting votes points to robust debate within these policy committees about the appropriate stance of monetary policy. That impression is reinforced by the ample evidence of dissenting views on the macro outlook in the published comments of individual members.

The pattern of votes tells a different story: the differences of opinion over the appropriate level of the policy rate between the majority and the dissenting members are almost without exception of no major economic significance. This is a puzzle. How could nine economists consistently keep coming up with essentially the same answer given the huge uncertainty involved in the calibration of the appropriate level of the policy rate – and in particular, nine economists who we know, based on their public remarks, periodically disagree over the macro outlook?

This chapter does not provide a definitive explanation for this puzzle. Nor does it take a stand on whether what amounts to a perma-consensus in the votes on the current level of Bank Rate ('Groupvote') is a good or bad thing. The objective of this chapter is more modest: to identify possible explanations for these interesting features of the voting record as a contribution to the broader debate about the decision-making process.

From the outset, we should be open about the fact that the current level of policy rate was never a summary statistic of the effective monetary stance, even in the pre-QE era. The transmission mechanism of monetary policy works through expectations of the decisions that policy committees will take in the future. So the disagreements over the macro outlook that are apparent in the speeches but not apparent in the votes on the current level of Bank Rate would presumably be reflected in material differences of view on the future path. But as we will go on to discuss, the Monetary Policy Committee (MPC) doesn't vote on the appropriate future path, nor does the committee appear keen to send a signal about that path or even debate it in any great detail.

Measuring Dissent: Incidence versus Extent

The committees that set monetary policy do not all operate the same way. It at least used to be the case that the MPC believed that it operated in a different way to many of its peers and that the frequency of dissenting votes proved it (King, 2007a, 2007b):

Disagreement among the Committee is inevitable; it is also desirable because it represents the individual judgements of members, rather than an attempt to create a false consensus. It is a source of strength. Over the past ten years, there have been 153 dissenting votes, on average more than one per meeting. This institutional encouragement of open debate is in contrast to many other central banks. We don't 'do consensus', as one former member put it. Dissent is more frequent than on other central bank committees which publish individual votes, and is not just token. . . . . Not only is the number of dissenting votes greater on the MPC, the frequency of more substantive disagreement – where one quarter or more of the voters dissented – is markedly greater.

Some of the other central banks have a token dissent, or one odd ball, but what this is saying is, 'no, we're markedly different' in that a significant amount of dissent is normal. That reflects the fact that this is genuinely a committee in which people feel under great pressure to say what they really think and that's the principal part of how the committee operates. That you get better decisions if you ask the nine people to say what they really think, instead of asking them to sit round and try and come to a consensus.

But does the *incidence* of dissent tell the whole story? Is it the right metric to judge whether the MPC 'does consensus' or not? One could instead look at the *extent* of the dissent in the votes, where we find an interesting result. Dissenting votes are almost without exception 25 basis points from the majority view in the Committee. Of course, Bank Rate is either left on hold or adjusted by 25 basis points at a typical policy meeting. There were 50 basis point "dove-ish" dissenting votes by a couple of MPC members at four of the meetings between November 2022 and June 2023 (a period when inflation was in double digit territory, the MPC saw "considerable uncertainties around the outlook") but Bank Rate was raised by at least 50 basis points at each of those meetings.

The obvious way to quantify the economic significance of a 25-basis point difference of opinion on the policy rate is to translate that difference into an implied difference in view on what the MPC ultimately cares about:

inflation. The simplest way to do that is to assume that all members use the same model of the economy to calibrate their vote on the policy rate.

According to the Committee's own estimate of the monetary transmission mechanism (MPC, 1999), a 25-basis point difference in the level of Bank Rate that is sustained for a year translates into a change in the rate of inflation two years into the future of perhaps at most 10 basis points. It is not surprising then that Willem Buiter once described the effect of a 25-basis point change as 'chicken feed'. At the margin, one might argue that the transmission mechanism has diminished over time: changes in the policy rate may have a smaller impact on inflation these days either because inflation is less sensitive to demand or demand is less sensitive to changes in the policy rate. If that is the case, then the 25-basis point dissent we see in the present day would amount to less than Buiter's chicken feed.

The 10-basis point difference at two years can also be compared to the perceived uncertainty about the rate of inflation at that time horizon. The central mass of the typical inflation fan chart reveals that the Committee believes that there is typically a 30% chance that inflation sits within an interval of around a percentage point in width and a 60% chance that it sits in a wider interval of more than two percentage points at that horizon. In other words, the Committee's collective uncertainty about the level of inflation dwarfs the differences of view on inflation implicit in the typical dissenting vote.

Explanations for the Lack of Major Dissent

In the rest of this chapter we review four explanations for our puzzle: the lack of meaningful dissent that we observe in the votes despite the periodic divergence of views that is apparent in the public comments of policymakers: groupthink (they all agree); gradualism (dissent emerges through a series of small steps); a desire to protect the signal sent by the majority; and concerns that major dissent would damage the reputation of the institution or the individual.

Groupthink

One possible explanation for the clustering of votes is groupthink. If you think almost exactly the same way as the other members of the committee then you should vote almost exactly the same way too. However, although the decision-making process within the Bank has led to some concerns about the risk of groupthink, there is at least one very good reason to question whether it can explain the observed clustering of votes.

A decision on Bank Rate will depend on an assessment of the macro outlook, which in turn reflects a series of judgement on the current structure and state of the economy, and an understanding of the loss function that guides policy decision. Indeed, as we will go on to discuss, even judgements about the nature of the uncertainty around those key judgements on the economy can have an impact on monetary strategy. It therefore seems unlikely that nine economists could arrive at almost exactly the same policy prescription if they each had to independently reach a conclusion on all the key judgements that are required to construct a view on the macro outlook or the loss function. It seems highly unlikely that nine economists could continuously perform this feat over and over again.

Of course, this is not what happens. The nine MPC members do not interrogate the data and form conclusions in private. MPC members all receive the same briefing from Bank staff. They sit in the same meetings and discuss the data and the staff's analysis of it and then debate the outlook together. There is one forecast round, not nine running in parallel. It is therefore not such a surprise that MPC members think in very similar ways. But it is something of a surprise that new members to the Committee think in very similar ways as their long-standing colleagues. These newcomers will not have participated in the many meetings and discussions that took place in previous forecast rounds before they joined the MPC when the other established members of the MPC supposedly reached that shared assessment of the state and structure of the economy. The newcomers nonetheless seem able to share in the conclusions of those discussions.

A good explanation should not solve one puzzle at the expense of creating an even bigger one. The groupthink thesis might explain the lack of meaningful dissent in the votes, but it raises an awkward question: if they vote the same way on monetary policy because they think the same way about the economy, then why don't they speak the same way about the economy?

The comments and speeches of MPC members point to clear differences of view on the macro outlook at various points in time – or to be more precise, differences of view that at least ought to translate into more than 25 basis points of dissent (Barwell, 2016). The on-the-record comments of MPC members present a direct challenge to the groupthink thesis.

Gradualism and the Iceberg of Dissent

Another way to rationalise the lack of significant dissent in the votes is that it reflects the same decision-making process that drives the intrinsic persistence or gradualism that we observe in the rate chosen by the majority. As Bernanke (2004) put it, '[a]s a general rule, the Federal Reserve tends to adjust interest rates incrementally, in a series of small or moderate steps in the same direction'. Dissent could emerge in exactly the same way: in a series of small steps.

The standard explanation for gradualism in the rate chosen by the majority is Brainard Uncertainty: the idea that it pays to take a conservative approach to setting policy in the face of uncertainty about the impact of your decisions on the economy. The logic is intuitive – you don't want to unnecessarily inject additional volatility into the economy – but it has long been known that uncertainty broadly defined does not always justify a conservative or gradualist approach. As Walsh (2000) concluded,

uncertainty comes in more than one flavour, and the appropriate policy response depends on the costs it imposes .... in some cases, policy should respond less strongly, while in others, it should respond more strongly ... Uncertainty is pervasive, but there is no one answer about how to deal with it.

To take one important example, Tetlow (2019) argues that uncertainty about inflation persistence in the economy should lead a central banker to be more aggressive in her response. So gradualism might explain moderate changes in the policy rate – and by extension, moderate dissent around the rate chosen by the majority – during certain periods and circumstances but not necessarily in all periods and all circumstances.

Nor is it clear that this 'uncertainty begets gradualism' thesis necessarily fits the facts in the voting record. Blinder (1999) famously described the gradualist strategy as one in which you deliberately change policy by less than you think will ultimately be appropriate and then you pause to 'watch developments' before you deliver the additional change in the policy rate that you originally thought necessary so long as the 'things work out about as expected'. Given the lags involved – in the transmission mechanism of policy, in the publication of data and in the processing of information by the policymaker – that pause could be quite long. It is not immediately obvious that one would know whether things were working out as expected from one meeting to the next or one forecast round to the next – which is what we need to fit the facts of a sequence of policy adjustments at that frequency.

To be fair, there are other conventional justifications for gradualism in the policy rate, aside from uncertainty. We shall return to one other popular argument later on: that policymakers might want to establish a track record of moving the policy rate gradually in order to gain greater traction on long rates (Woodford, 2003). Stein and Sunderman (2018) highlight another: that policymakers might be concerned about the financial stability implications of the excessive volatility in asset prices that large moves in the policy rate might create. In any case, as Bernanke observes, while the literature generally suggests that central banks should be gradualist, it is not clear that, say, the Federal Reserve actually has been (e.g. see Sack, 2000; Rudebusch, 2006).

If gradualism works as an explanation for the behaviour of the policy rate chosen by the majority, then perhaps it might also explain the dynamics of the votes of individual members. Dissenting members may be consistently making a conscious decision not to vote for what they believe to be the 'optimal' level of the policy rate. Instead – to paraphrase Blinder – they may be voting for a modest change in the direction of that optimal rate and then pausing to watch developments in the expectation that they will continue to adjust their vote in the direction of that optimal rate if things work out as they – and not the majority – expect.

The dissenting votes we observe should therefore be understood as the tip of the iceberg of dissent, with only the first step in what will turn out to be a gradual divergence in the desired rate path visible to the outside world. Gradualism can reconcile the dispersion of views we find in the speeches of policymakers with the lack of dispersion in the votes. The comments of dissenting MPC members implicitly reflect the submerged part of that iceberg too. However, there are still awkward questions to resolve for the gradualism thesis.

For a start, if we are to accept this explanation then it would be nice to find evidence that MPC members believe in these arguments. For example, it would be reassuring to find examples of dissenting members deploying arguments along the following lines in the minutes, speeches or parliamentary testimony: 'I profoundly disagree with the majority on the state of the economy but I will only vote for a marginal change because I believe these happen to be circumstances in which uncertainty demands a gradualist approach or I am concerned about excess volatility in the bond market.' We don't see those arguments.

Gradualism might provide a neat explanation for why there is no significant dissent in the votes at a particular point in time, but it is harder to explain why there is not significant dissent at any point in time. After all, each member is supposedly planning to gradually adjust their vote towards what they perceive to be the optimal rate as they receive confirmation from the data flow that they have the right call on the economy. But token dissent never evolves into significant dissent, which implies that all members of the committee must be more or less learning exactly the same lessons from the data when they pause to watch developments. We should expect members to learn similar lessons: they are sat in the same building, monitoring the same data flow with support from the same staff. But it is hard to explain why there are so few examples of members even managing to reach the second step on the path of dissent – that is, a 50-basis point dissent.

Ultimately, there is a fundamental difference between the gradualism argument applied to a committee as a whole and to a dissenting member. The gradualist committee at least takes the policy rate a step in the right direction. That is not the case for dissenting members. The policy rate will only even gradually start adjusting to the optimal rate once he or she is able to persuade the majority around to taking the first step on a different path. Until that point, dissenting members will perceive that the policy stance is stuck in the wrong place.

Worse still, if policymakers are only ever willing to register token dissent in the votes (25 basis points) then they can even become a hostage to the majority. Dissenting gradualists might find that they feel compelled to vote for changes in the policy stance in the wrong direction. Imagine for a second that the majority is gradually raising the policy rate through a sequence of 25 basis point changes. If a dissenting member wants to keep her vote at most 25 basis points from the majority view then he or she will also have to keep voting for 25-basis point increases as well to prevent a larger margin of dissent opening up. This may sound like an implausible scenario, but it is arguably not a bad description of what actually happened to Lars Svensson during the period when the Riksbank was raising rates around a decade ago. We will return to how Svensson solved this problem in due course.

Negotiation Strategy?

Another possible explanation for the lack of material dissent in the votes when there does appear to be material dissent in the views is that it reflects a negotiation tactic. MPC members care about getting the monetary stance in the right place. They may feel that they are more likely to persuade other members of the committee to change their minds (and their votes) if they advocate for a sequence of small changes, as opposed to one large change. In other words, dissenting members are consistently making a conscious decision to self-censor their votes.

This negotiating tactic has its limitations. Even in the best-case scenario – in which a dissenting member successfully advocates for a sequence of marginal changes in the same direction to ultimately achieve the required change in the stance – the policy rate crawls towards the level preferred by the dissenting member. Nonetheless, dissenting members might believe that this is still the most effective way to achieve a major shift in the debate and the votes within the committee. If you cannot jump, you have to crawl.

One problem with this argument – and indeed many of these explanations – is that it seems plausible as an explanation for how some policymakers behave, some of the time. What is less plausible is that it applies to all members, all of the time. If negotiation tactics is the reason why we see token dissent in the votes then it is a little strange that not a single dissenting member once decided to try an alternative strategy and vote for a larger change in policy to see what impact that had on the views and votes of others.

It is also worth noting that dissenting members typically do not go to any effort to hide their ultimate objective from the rest of the committee. Most dissenting member do not self-censor their views on the macroeconomic outlook even if they self-censor their votes. It should therefore be obvious to the majority that the dissenting member wants a major shift in the policy stance even if they only appear to be voting for a minor change this month.

Damaging the Signal and Following in Svensson's Footsteps

Alternatively, policymakers may choose to censor their views for fear that major dissent in the votes could damage the signal that the majority want to send about the path of interest rates.

Monetary policy influences asset prices and ultimately demand and inflation primarily via the expectations of the decisions that the policy committee will take in the future rather than via the decision it took at the last meeting (the prevailing level of the policy rate). The signal that a committee sends about future policy decisions is therefore a powerful lever which can aid the pursuit of price stability by shifting those expectations.

It makes perfect sense that the majority within a policy committee should want to send a clear message to the markets. It is plausible that major dissent in the votes could distract attention away from that message. The media and the markets might then focus too much on the reasons why one or two members profoundly disagree with the majority rather than on the substance of the strategy favoured by the majority.

The signalling argument essentially says the minority choose to self-censor in the interests of the majority, perhaps because in a repeated game, most members expect to be in the majority, most of the time. Indeed, if we embrace Woodford's rationale for gradualism highlighted above, then there is a collective interest in gradualism that provides current and future majorities with greater leverage on long rates.

The first problem with this signalling argument is that revealed preference suggests that the MPC has never attached that much importance to sending clear signals to the market about the future path of rates. The MPC has consistently chosen not to publish a rate path to guide market expectations of the future path of policy. It is hard to imagine that dissenting members are worried about damaging the signal that the majority are trying to send when there is no clear signal to speak of, and presumably a belief within the institution that sending such a signal would be a bad idea.

The second problem with this argument is that it requires dissenting members to always focus on the long game and follow a precedent that serves the interests of the current majority, presumably because they expect to be in the majority at some point in the future. In the here and now, dissenting members should not want the media and the markets to focus exclusively on the majority signal because they disagree with it. The Woodford doctrine does not say that you follow a gradualist approach to gain traction on long rates even if you think you are heading in the wrong direction!

As with many of these arguments, it is easy to imagine some dissenting members reaching the conclusion some of the time that it is better not to damage the signal of the majority, but it is a little harder to explain why all of them – across several decades – always reach the same conclusion. We might also ask: who explains this argument to newcomers on the MPC?

The third problem with this signalling argument is that it relies on the belief that the market doesn't attach any importance to the remarks of dissenting members, whether that be in a paragraph in the minutes, in testimony to parliamentarians or in speeches. Otherwise, the markets would understand that dissenting members are sending an implicit signal of their own, hinting at the true extent of their dissent. So, if concern about damaging the signal sent by the majority was the reason why policymakers consistently choose not to register meaningful dissent in the votes, then why do they continue to hint at meaningful dissent in their speeches? And, if the answer is that nobody attaches any importance to those remarks and speeches, then why bother?

In theory, a dissenting member can do more than just hint at the true extent of their dissent. They can describe it by publishing their own view of the appropriate path for the policy rate that builds from the token dissent that is apparent in the votes into a material difference of view on the level of rates in the future. This is precisely what Lars Svensson did when he was in the minority (Svensson, 2016):

In their review of Riksbank monetary policy, Goodfriend and King make a big point of the minority (Karolina Ekholm and me) having voted for policy rates only 0.25 percentage point below the majority and use that to argue that the rate hikes 2010-2011 were 'broadly accepted by all members of Executive Board'. But they fail to report that the monetary policy stance, appropriately measured, that the minority voted for was substantially more expansionary than the majority's (not to speak of that it was only a first step of several needed in a move toward a better monetary policy). They thus fail to report the position of the minority correctly. For instance, in September 2011, the minority voted for a policy stance equivalent to a repo rate 1.5 percentage point lower the next 4 quarters than the majority's stance.

There is nothing to stop dissenting MPC members following in Svensson's footsteps. They could frame their views on the appropriate path for policy relative to the path currently expected by market participants, which after all determines the effective monetary stance.

Reputational Considerations – for the Group and for the Individual

The final candidate explanation for the lack of material dissent in the votes is a concern about reputation. That is, MPC members choose not to register a major dissenting vote on the policy rate because they believe it would either damage the reputation of the institution or their own personal reputation.

It is not unreasonable to assume that MPC members might be concerned that major dissent in the vote on interest rates could somehow damage the reputation of the MPC or Bank. There is potential path dependence here: the more time passes and the more that the voting record is dominated by dissent of plus or minus 25 basis points, the more shocking a vote of plus or minus 100 basis points might be.

However, we should not forget the dissent that we find in the public comments of MPC members. So this variant of the reputation argument relies on the idea that policymakers disagreeing on the interest rate decision is profoundly shocking and potentially damaging to the institution, but policymakers disagreeing over the economic outlook that should drive the interest rate decision is not. The reader may believe that this is a reasonable description of the world: economists are expected to disagree about economics, but central bankers are not expected to have profound disagreements over the policy rate. Nonetheless, it would be interesting to know how every dissenting member of the committee reached this conclusion: that major dissent in the votes would damage the institution but dissent in the speeches does not.

It is also possible that MPC members might systematically choose to censor their dissent in the votes for personal reputational reasons. That is, MPC members may subscribe to the Keynes doctrine that the world is not kind to those who fail unconventionally so there is a risk involved in registering genuine dissent that turns out after the fact to have been in error. Once again, the more time passes and the more the voting record is dominated by dissent of plus or minus 25 basis points, the more unconventional a dissent of say 100 basis points looks. This argument relies on the fact that there is nothing unconventional and no reputational risk involved in publishing a speech where you radically disagree with the majority about some aspect of the outlook. Perhaps the content of speeches is soon forgotten but the voting record endures.

It is also worth reflecting on why personal reputation matters to MPC members. One reasonable hypothesis is that a reputation for having poor calls on the economy could influence job prospects and future earnings once an individual leaves the committee. If that is the case then one might expect this mechanism to be more powerful for those who expect to work within financial markets once they leave the committee and less powerful for, say, established academics, and particularly those whose research interests lie outside monetary economics. However, neither group seems inclined to register major dissent in the votes.

A Technical Consideration

Finally, it is worth acknowledging a possible technical reason which might explain why we don't see major dissent in the votes. Dissenting members might be unsure how to calibrate the appropriate size of a significant jump in the policy rate. Again, this may sound far-fetched, but Svensson (2014) argues that it was an issue at the Riksbank:

Why could I not dissent in favour of a single large step directly to an 'optimal' policy rate and policy-rate path? This was because of technical limitations in the methods available at the Riksbank to calculate alternative policy-rate paths and corresponding inflation and unemployment forecasts. The methods only allowed small variations from the 'main scenario', that is, the majority's policy-rate path and forecasts. This meant that my policy-rate paths in practice only showed that the majority's path was not optimal and in what direction the policy-rate should be adjusted, not how much it needed to be adjusted, in order to be optimal.

It is unclear whether MPC members have the resources at their disposal to calculate the size of that large step to the optimal policy rate in the event of a dissenting view. What is clear is that if they do, nobody has been willing to deploy them to express major dissent in the vote on Bank Rate.

Conclusion

This chapter has highlighted a number of potential explanations for the apparent disconnect between the votes and the views of dissenting members of the MPC. None of them are particularly satisfactory. The obvious way to establish which, if any, of these explanations are relevant is to ask former members of the committee what they think. There remains a compelling case for producing an oral history of the MPC if we want to understand how and why committees function in practice.

References

Barwell, Richard (2016), 'Nine votes, one view and the never-ending consensus on the MPC during the great stability', in J. Chadha, A Chrystal, J. Pearlman, P. Smith and S. Wright (eds.), *The UK Economy in the Long Expansion and Its Aftermath*, Cambridge University Press.

Barwell, Richard (2019), 'Inertial groupvote', in Richard Barwell and Jagjit Chadha (eds.), *Renewing Our Monetary Vows: Open Letters to the Governor of the Bank of England*. National Institute of Economic and Social Research, Occasional Paper No. 58.

Bernanke, Ben (2004), 'Gradualism', Remarks by Governor Ben S. Bernanke at an economics luncheon co-sponsored by the Federal Reserve Bank of San Francisco (Seattle Branch) and the University of Washington, Seattle, Washington, 20 May.

Blinder, Alan (2004), *The Quiet Revolution: Central Banking Goes Modern*. Yale University Press.

Blinder, Alan (1999), *Central Banking in Theory and Practice*. MIT Press.

King, Mervyn (2007a), 'The MPC ten years on', lecture by Mr Mervyn King, Governor of the Bank of England, to the Society of Business Economists, London, 2 May.

King, Mervyn (2007b), Interview with *Financial Times*, 3 May.

MPC (1999), The transmission mechanism of monetary policy, *Bank of England Quarterly Bulletin*, Q2, May.

Rudebusch, Glenn (2006), 'Monetary policy inertia: Fact or fiction?' *International Journal of Central Banking*. 2(4), 85–135.

Sack, Brian (2000), 'Does the Fed act gradually? A VAR analysis', *Journal of Monetary Economics*. 46(1), 229–56.

Stein, Jeremy and Adi Sunderam (2018), 'The Fed, the bond market, and gradualism in monetary policy', *Journal of Finance*. 73(3), 1015–60.

Svensson, Lars (2014), 'Major differences between the majority and minority of the Riksbank Executive Board', Mimeo.

Svensson, Lars (2016), 'Goodfriend and king misreport the monetary policy stance of the minority', Mimeo.

Tetlow, Robert (2019), 'The monetary policy response to uncertain inflation persistence', *Economics Letters*. 175, 5–8.

Walsh, Chris (2000), 'Uncertainty and monetary policy', *FRBSF Economic Letter* 2000–08.

Woodford, Michael (2003), 'Optimal monetary policy inertia', *Review of Economic Studies*. 70, 861–86.

V

Lessons for Central Bank Independence

13 The MPC
Then and Now

Mervyn King

I am delighted to join you at this Money, Macro and Finance Society Conference. And I am especially pleased that we are meeting in the Sibson Building. Robin Sibson, who was vice-chancellor of this university between 1994 and 2001, was a distinguished mathematician and statistician. I got to know him when we overlapped at King's College, Cambridge. His untimely death was a loss to many, and I am glad that his contributions have been commemorated in this award-winning building.

I have been asked to speak on the topic of lessons learnt from 25 years of the Monetary Policy Committee (MPC). I'm tempted to wonder whether, in light of recent events, we should rename this: lessons forgotten from 25 years of the MPC.

But there is also much to remember. I attended and voted at 194 meetings of the MPC between the first meeting in June 1997 and my last in June 2013, a record that is very unlikely to be broken. So my reflections may still be useful because they span the history of the MPC and its creation.

And I think it's important to remember what used to happen before the creation of the MPC, and I want to do that by contrasting two meetings to set interest rates, one before and one after the creation of the MPC.

The first was the last monthly meeting in 1997 under the then Chancellor Ken Clarke, which took place during the election campaign in 1997. This was the last of what became known as the Ken and Eddie shows, in which the chancellor took the decisions and the Bank gave public advice. It took place at the Inland Revenue offices in Nottingham because we were in the middle of an election campaign, and it was made clear at the outset at the meeting that there wouldn't be any change in interest rates for political reasons. But it might be useful, having given that verdict, to hear the evidence. And that's what happened. It turned out to be, of course, more of a pleasant occasion to say goodbye to Ken Clarke.

Now contrast that with the meeting of the MPC a decade later at 12 noon on Thursday, 10 May 2007. Tony Blair announced his resignation as prime minister after ten years at number 10. At exactly the same time, at 12 noon, the Bank announced a 25-basis point increase in interest rates. Nothing could symbolise more, the change in the monetary regime than the contrast between the two meetings. Before independence of the Bank of England, it would have been inconceivable that interest rates would have risen on a day when there was an important government announcement.

But let me start at the beginning. I want to go back to the 1970s because the combination of an intellectual error plus bad luck led to very significant inflation during the 1970s. The error was to believe that there was a permanent trade-off between inflation and output. By tolerating a higher inflation rate, unemployment, it was thought, could be held at a lower level. And the bad luck was the arrival of two oil price shocks. And that combination led to high inflation, peaking at 27% in the UK in 1975.

Several central banks in response to all this were rather cautious about combating inflation. But two central banks set out to keep inflation down, despite the size of these supply shocks, the Bundesbank and the Swiss National Bank. These two countries experienced not only lower inflation but also smaller recessions than countries with central banks that were more cautious. The Great Inflation was very painful to eradicate. But it did create a constituency for price stability. And that's one big difference, perhaps now from then.

Efforts to bring down inflation in the 1980s rested on, first, the use of monetary and, secondly, exchange rate targets. But no one doubted the importance of reducing inflation. Reliance was placed on targets for the monetary aggregates in the first half of the 1980s, and in the second half, policy was focused on implicit and then explicit targets for the exchange rate of sterling against the Deutschmark.

Both of these approaches came unstuck largely, I think, because of what we might call non-stationarity. There were significant changes in financial regulation in the early 1980s, which altered the relationship between inflation and the monetary aggregates. And then in the later 1980s, German reunification altered the appropriateness of trying to link sterling to the Deutschmark. And with the benefit of hindsight, you might well argue that the tightness of monetary policy was probably better indicated by the exchange rate in the early 1980s and by monetary aggregates towards the end of the decade, the reverse of the measures used for policy purposes at the time.

I joined the Bank of England in 1991, and interest rate changes then could occur at any time on any day of the week. I could be sitting at my desk and receive a phone call before lunch saying that the Chancellor would like a meeting to discuss interest rates after lunch. Well, there would just be time to cobble together a few numbers and an anecdote or two before setting off to the Treasury. If a budget in that era was well-received by the markets, to use the expression that was common at the time, then the government would reward itself with an interest rate cut.

The timing of decisions was heavily influenced by political factors such as by-elections, and prime ministers were always conscious of the desirability from their point of view of cuts in interest rates. There was nothing systematic about the process of setting interest rates. So it's not surprising that two chancellors during this period, Nigel Lawson and Norman Lamont, tried to persuade – unsuccessfully – their respective prime ministers of the merits of bank independence. Now, all of this is crucial, I think, because we've moved into a period in which the academic literature has forgotten the political climate in which interest rates decisions were made.

One of the enormous contributions of the MPC is simply to make interest rate decisions a systematic process reflecting the needs of the economy. And that, in many ways, is perhaps its most important contribution.

The key decade in the movement towards independence and the creation of the MPC was, of course, the 1990s, with the arrival of inflation targets and a belief that the process of setting interest rates was central to controlling inflation. Intermediate targets had fallen victim to non-stationarity, and so it seemed to make sense to express policy in terms of the final objective, namely inflation. In other words, to adopt an inflation target. Two developments accelerated the case for bank independence. The first was the success of the inflation target and the related Bank of England's Inflation Report, which was first published in February 1993. In raising the level of debate about monetary policy and establishing the bank's credibility in making policy judgements, the Ken and Eddie show, with Ken Clarke as chancellor and Eddie George as governor, was a natural precursor to independence. The second factor was a conference to celebrate the bank's tercentenary in 1994, where the American and Israeli economist Stan Fischer presented a paper in which he argued the merits of central bank independence. And I think from then on the subject of independence was openly and widely discussed and debated. The Bank was very careful not to lobby for independence. But Tony Blair and Gordon Brown in opposition took soundings from business leaders at home and people like Alan Greenspan overseas. And independence was to usher in a regime of systematic decision processes and predictable timing of announcements of decisions on interest rates.

And so we come to 1997 and the general election at the beginning of May. Gordon Brown entered the Treasury on the Friday afternoon, the day after the general election, with a draft letter to the Governor setting out the terms of full Bank of England independence in respect of interest rates. The Treasury worked in secret over the weekend, and the plan was launched to an unsuspecting Bank on the bank holiday Monday and then to an unsuspecting press at a press conference at 11 a.m. on Tuesday, 6 May.

Some journalists at that press conference didn't actually believe what the Chancellor was saying. Having announced that interest rate decisions would be handed to the Bank, the press then said, 'But you will be there, Chancellor, won't you?' And it took some time to persuade the press of the substance of what Gordon Brown had announced. When they were, they were astonished. If you look back at the newspapers of the time, you will see that the banner headlines, both the Evening Standard on the Tuesday afternoon and the press the next morning, on the front page showed that this was a real revolution in monetary policy. And I think what was most astonishing was that with the help of Paul Tucker and his team and my team in the economics area, within three weeks, the new MPC was set up, literally set up from nothing to an operational MPC process.

The process of the new meetings of the MPC started at the end of May, and the first full meeting with voting took place on 5–6 June 1997, when the committee voted to raise Bank Rate by 25 basis points to 6.5%. Before the election there had of course been discussions between the Bank and the Labour Party, initially with a dinner between two top teams. There were also quadrilateral meetings and then bilateral meetings between Eddie George and Gordon Brown. The Labour Party in opposition proposed a MPC, not in the context of independence but in the context of providing advice to the chancellor. And there was a great deal of debate about whether there should be voting on such a committee. Some in the Bank were absolutely against voting. And I can see why. We had some pretty heated discussions in the run-up to the election about how we would describe the process of decision making among a purely advisory MPC. And in those preparations we just reinforced our view that such a committee would be a halfway house. But at no time did we believe that Brown and Blair were contemplating announcing independence as the first act of the new government.

So when it came, it was a bolt out of the blue. Now, what happened after that? Well, during the first year, there was a good deal of criticism of the committee for having unanimous votes. People said that there was groupthink: we were simply all voting the same way, and there was no debate on the committee. That was just as unfair as the press coverage in the second year which started to criticise the Bank when there were split votes, for being a bunch of squabbling academics who couldn't agree on anything. And the same journalists made these two criticisms. But eventually, people got used to the idea that each member of the Committee had their own vote, their own view. They talked to each other. That's why we had a committee. They listened to each other. And at the end of the day, they cast their own vote. And during the time when I was in the Bank, when we would meet on Thursday morning to take our final decision, it was impossible to know what the outcome of the vote would be. And I think that is utterly different from almost any other central bank, including the Fed. People were allowed to give their own view, and the decision that was made was the result of majority voting among those nine members, and no one could anticipate where that would go.

Over 25 years, the MPC has, I think, proved a great success in institutional reform. Inflation averaged close to the 2% target, at least until 2021. People accepted that this was a good way of making technocratic judgements to meet a target set by parliament. One of the things I recall during my MPC period was that as we went around the country, and everyone on the MPC would visit different parts of the UK, I would meet business people who might say after a discussion, 'Well, I don't really agree with the decision you made at the last meeting, but I'm very happy that the MPC is making the decision because all the arguments I would have made were made at the meeting, and they're in the minutes. So I knew that the case I would have pressed was put to the committee.'

So let me now come to my conclusions. I want to draw five main lessons from the experience of the MPC, which I think are really very important. The first one is that inflation targeting is not a new theory of inflation or the monetary transmission mechanism. It just isn't. And that's where the recent literature is going very badly wrong. Like any successful diet, the process of inflation targeting by the MPC is continuous and indefinite. It tries to steer away from boom and bust just as a successful diet is not an alternation between binge and starvation. It's a way of living for central banks that you can keep going indefinitely.

Unfortunately, the academic profession has turned a way of life into a precise and rather hubristic view that central banks can closely control inflation. And this has led, I think, to serious mistakes in 2020 and 2021, where instead of asking the question, what is going on in the economy, central banks fell back on the models. And they concluded that a large fall in output was akin to a business cycle recession, only bigger than normal. So they did a lot of QE to support the economy. They forgot that, unlike a normal business cycle, potential supply had fallen. In those circumstances it was strange to think of boosting demand. Belatedly, Jay Powell said on 26 August at Jackson Hole, '[W]e are taking forceful and rapid steps to moderate demand so that it comes into better alignment with supply, and to keep inflation expectations anchored.' Now, this is not rocket science. There was a time when textbooks said inflation reflects the fact that too much money is chasing too few goods. Well, Covid-19 guaranteed that there were too few goods, but then central banks managed to create too much money. That common sense, which is really first year economics, should have guided policy in 2020 and 2021. And the reason it didn't, I think, is that central banks have become rather captive to a particular academic view of how to think about monetary policy.

The second lesson is that money matters. It's bizarre for a central bank to stop thinking in terms of money when inflation is a nominal phenomenon. You just can't explain inflation in a model with only real variables. The attempt to do so by assuming that inflation can be explained solely by expectations which in turn are driven solely by the inflation target is an example not only of a loss of common sense but also a failure of imagination. It's totally circular reasoning. If you have an inflation target and you say, 'What drives inflation in the medium term? Well, the inflation target does so we needn't worry about it' then you are assuming that any deviation of inflation from target is always transitory. When we were doing simulations on the model in the Bank of England in the early days of the MPC, whatever policy path we assumed, inflation always came back to 2%. Why? Because the model said it had to. That's why we didn't want to rely on a single model. Quantitative easing is electronic money printing, boosting broad money by a substantial amount. In the US, broad money in 2021 was growing at the fastest rate since World War II. In the UK, M4 growth peaked in February 2021 at 15.5%. It has come down a lot since, which also suggests that people ought to think carefully about what's going to happen in the next two years. But the fact that people didn't even ask the question – what does this mean? – is odd.

The third lesson follows, I think from the first two, which is set policy in the world and not in a model. Forward guidance was introduced around 2013 and 2014, and in my view it has not been successful. It's not time consistent. There is something very weird about the idea that you can predict where you think interest rates will be three years from now, particularly in a point forecast, which is what you see in the US Federal Reserve's dot-plots.

The problem was that in a difficult situation where growth was slowing, and inflation was close to but probably a bit below target, people were desperate to find new policy instruments. But saying what you think you will do three years from now is not a policy instrument. It's a statement of where you think the policy instrument will be set. And you can't possibly have the information available today to know coherently where rates will be. You would change your mind about where rates will go according to the data. And I think this belief that you could pretend that there was a model in which forward guidance seemed to work and a model in which all kinds of fancy gimmicks seemed to be a good idea reached its peak in August 2020, when the Federal Reserve introduced, at the worst possible time, a regime of asymmetric average inflation targeting. We can control inflation so precisely that we are going to offset the cumulative under-shoot of inflation below 2% in the last few years by allowing inflation to go over 2% for a while and then bring it back. That was clearly hubris, and it looks even more so today.

The fourth lesson is to abandon point forecasts. The early MPC did abandon point forecasts. We refused to make forecasts saying that infla-tion will be 3.4% next year, 4.1% the year after and so on. We wanted to talk about risks, and we deliberately constructed the fan charts which the Bank pioneered in such a way that we did not reveal a mean or central view because we wanted people to focus on the dispersion in the chart and on the risks to the outlook. That is a sensible way to communicate policy. It's not sensible to make point forecasts. And I think that in recent years the MPC has slipped back into slightly bad habits in this respect.

And the last, the fifth, lesson is focuses on trying to understand the real equilibrium or disequilibrium of the economy. What's going on in the economy? Most models don't do this, nor should they. The whole point of a model is to have a simplification of the world in such a way that you can get your head around one narrow problem. And most of the models which are being used to think about monetary policy are drastic simplifications of what's happening in the world and for good reason. They are helpful in providing intuition about certain ideas. But they are not a description of the world. So whatever view you take about the consequences of the secular fall in long-term real interest rates since 1990, whether you think there's a problem of secular stagnation or that low real interest rates represent a new equilibrium, such questions must be posed and answered in order to set policy. But they can't be answered in the context of most of the models that are being used to construct monetary policy at present.

So those are the five big lessons: inflation targeting is a way of living, not a theory of the monetary transmission mechanism; money matters; set policy in the world, not in a model; abandon point forecasts; and finally understand the real equilibrium or disequilibrium of the economy.

Let me conclude with an example of a successful MPC policy response to supply side shocks, not dissimilar to the challenge the Bank is facing today. From the middle of 2007 until the end of 2008, the sterling effective exchange rate fell by 25%. That is the largest fall in the sterling exchange rate in the post-war period. It was bound to lead to a significant rise, not just in import prices but in the price level of tradeable goods and services. Assuming that non-tradable goods and services prices remained constant, then the domestic price level would rise by somewhere in the region of 8 to 12 percentage points, a huge figure. And at a time of recession, we decided to accommodate that increase, provided that domestically generated inflation remained stable. And that meant allowing inflation to run above target for around 3 to 4 years. The cumulative overshoot of inflation above target from the start of the depreciation to 2013 was around seven percentage points.

After that, inflation, as we had said it would, did return to target and that achievement of accommodating a large depreciation of the currency without destabilising inflation expectations is, in my view, one of the major achievements of the new regime of central bank independence and inflation targeting. So the lesson is that one can accommodate supply shocks, provided that domestically generated inflation is held under control. And the problem we face today is that core inflation, domestically generated inflation, has risen quite significantly because of the monetary injection in 2020 and 2021.

Inflation targeting and the creation of the MPC have changed the way decisions are taken. They have proved to be a necessary but not sufficient condition for price stability.

The recent inflation stems from mistaken ideas promulgated by theorists who've persuaded central banks to set policy in the model and not in the world. I don't think we should blame individuals or even central banks for the recent mistakes. They reflect flawed economic thinking. But after 25 years, I think the MPC is a good way of making monetary policy, and it's here to stay.

14 Outlines of a Reform Programme for the UK's Monetary Regime

Paul Tucker

The title of this session is 'Lessons from 25 Years of the Monetary Policy Committee'. Trying to get to the nub of things, I'm going to ask what one would now change in the Monetary Policy Committee (MPC) set-up. That question gets some urgency, or at least salience, from the malaise that monetary authorities seem currently to be in across the Western world.[1]

Before turning to the substance, I want, for purposes of disclosure, to begin by recording my own involvement in the path to Bank of England independence. I was private secretary to Governor Leigh-Pemberton when, in the early 1990s, inflation targeting was introduced. This happened partly because Mervyn, who just spoke, was quickly ready with an alternative regime after the UK fell out of Europe's Exchange Rate Mechanism and partly because Chancellor of the Exchequer Norman Lamont backed a regime that would give a much bigger and more overt role to the Bank – absolutely and, crucially, relative to Treasury mandarins – since its analysis and forecasts would be published. In at least one private speech, Leigh-Pemberton had expressly described Exchange Rate Mechanism membership as a substitute for independence (and the credibility it could bring to Britain's monetary regime). So the thought of independence was very much alive in the Bank. A few years before, Chancellor of the Exchequer Nigel Lawson had proposed it to Prime Minister Margaret Thatcher. And George Blunden, who had come out of retirement in the mid-1980s to be Deputy Governor, ended his very last speech by saying the country needed independence but it should not happen until the country was ready for it.

A few years later, after a spell on open-market operations and government debt management (quite useful for designing quantitative easing (QE) operations), I was the head of Monetary Assessment and Strategy division when the MPC was created. Unlike my bosses, when I saw the

---

[1] With thanks to David Aikman, Richard Barwell, Charlie Bean and Steve Cecchetti for exchanges on earlier drafts.

size of the Labour majority, I did think the new Labour government would introduce independence quickly because that was the rational thing for them to do. Anyway, I supported Mervyn in the face-to-face negotiations on the regime's details with Alan Budd and Stephen Pickford at the Treasury. I then took the minutes of the MPC alongside two other colleagues for five years and, finally, in 2002, became a member of the MPC for over a decade.

Is the Malaise Rooted in Models or Incentives?

Mervyn has talked about the hazards of relying mechanically on models. I completely agree and, for what it is worth, that was his view (and not only his) when he chaired the MPC, as it had been Eddie George's beforehand. During those years – the Committee's first 16 years – a not uncommon refrain when presented with model outputs was along the lines of 'But we do not believe that. It cannot be so because xyz.' Looking back, I think that helpfully shaped the incentives of the staff. They had to come to forecast meetings not only with the outputs of the main forecasting model but also with a story about the economic outlook and with a series of puzzles that they thought relevant to the committee's formation of its own views and its policy decisions.

The Anchor Is the Committee Itself

Part of the challenge with blind adherence to modern macroeconomic models is that they are typically used in ways that assume the nominal target – in Britain's case, the inflation target – is fully credible, meaning that long-term inflation expectations are anchored to the target. This introduces the monetary equivalent of Newton's force of gravity: however great the shock, inflation will tend back to the target.

There are two problems with this. The first, and obviously the greatest, is that articulation of a monetary regime, however well done, cannot possibly do all the work. As with political constitutions, the regime documents are mere parchment. The true anchor is the committee itself.

The second problem underlines that. If a model assumes credibility, the policy question of how to respond to a particular shock becomes how to find the best path for interest rates after weighing the costs of volatility in inflation, volatility in economic activity (including jobs), and whatever else is deemed germane to the welfare analysis. But if the anchor is something to be earned (continuously) rather than a God-given right, that framing of policy's job is profoundly misleading. Instead, the policy challenge is how to achieve all those welfare-efficiency things without endangering the anchor or even in ways that re-establish the anchor.

The import of all this is that everything – repeat, everything – a country's monetary authority says and does must be directed towards reaffirming the credibility of the anchor, which is to say the authority's credibility. Casually shrugging off inflationary (or deflationary) risks in the face of a big shock is costly loose talk. A stark example is the Federal Reserve's dismissal of upside risks to inflation after the 2021 fiscal stimulus. Even if it had been reasonable to regard the most likely outlook as benign, it was hard to maintain that the risks to inflation were symmetric rather than skewed to the upside. That matters to the extent that policy does best to feedback from the mean of the distribution or, alternatively, to head off plausible serious risks. So the deeper point is not about models but about processes, or people and processes, or something like that.

All that being so, the incentives of monetary policymakers could hardly matter more. I have come to worry that something important happened in the aftermath of the Global Financial Crisis (GFC), manifested in politicians trying to reorient the incentives of monetary policymakers. In a nutshell, during 2009–11 the business of maintaining low and stable inflation might have ended up looking easier than it is. That mattered because, during the crisis, the central banks had revealed the extent of their latent fiscal capabilities. In particular, they had introduced facilities designed to steer the allocation of bank lending towards the real economy; the widely emulated Bank's Funding for Lending Scheme did just that (insofar as the real economy was favoured over financial market traders etc.). But if central bankers can steer the supply of credit during crises, why not get them to do that during financial peacetime – except now towards parts of the economy elected politicians (and their backers) want to favour, and away from parts of the economy they disfavour, such as polluters and so on.

In other words, if maintaining price stability seems easy, then elected politicians have powerful incentives to get central banks to make discretionary use of their latent fiscal instruments to pursue other goals. I think that is a mistake, and potentially a costly one, as it risks diluting or displacing the focus on the core mandate.[2] There is a question here about how to constrain political salami slicing of the regime – but also one about why independent central bankers would acquiesce.

---

[2] These arguments are at the heart of *Unelected Power*, where they are set out more clearly. After World War II, the Bank of England was actively involved in credit policy, but it was not then independent, being known colloquially as the operational arm of HMT. Independence changed that.

Incentives: Prestige and Esteem, but for What?

The standard case for independence is that, whatever their better thoughts, elected policymakers have almost overwhelming incentives to give more weight to short-run economic and financial booms than to their longer-term costs. But if delegation to an arm's-length authority, insulated from quotidian politics, is to do its work, it needs somehow to harness the incentives of the regime's stewards, who, after all, are all flesh and blood men and women.

A precondition for this – one opening up an illuminating perspective on central banks taking on more and more functions – is that appointed central bank leaders need to care (a lot) about the public prestige and professional esteem accrued from delivering the mandate, or foregone if they do not. Delegation to technocrats does not work without that harness.

So, if a central banker has a public reputation for combatting, say, climate change and inequality, or for other social justice causes, maybe they will not care so much about the opprobrium coming their way if (steady state) inflation rises under their watch.[3]

Among other things, this implies an independent central bank's mandate should be as narrow as possible, and its objectives should be both measurable and capable of being monitored by interested members of the public.[4]

Against the background of those general thoughts, we can move from principles and political science to some detailed proposals. There are a dozen.

As emphasized in *Unelected Power*,[5] it is important to distinguish the regime itself from the stewardship of the regime. In Britain, Parliament is responsible for the statutory regime; Treasury are responsible for matters delegated to them; and the MPC is responsible for matters delegated to them. So I am going to break my remarks down under those headings. Of course, the MPC regime is not the only regime entrusted to the Bank. But I will touch on the Bank's post-2010 responsibilities for financial stability only where helpful to illuminate a point about the MPC.

Finally, it is important to stress that for each proposal, the argument will be sketched rather than fully laid out.

---

[3] Having central banks take a leading role in combatting the incidence or costs of climate change, or inequality and other social issues, also risks diluting the incentives of elected governments to use their much broader set of instruments. But that is a different argument from the one explored in the main text.

[4] That sentiment and those of *Unelected Power* were captured in an early 2023 speech by the Fed chair. Powell (2023).

[5] Tucker (2018).

The Legislated Part of the Regime: Something to Keep, Something to Change

The most important part of Britain's monetary regime is found in statutory law. The legislation creates the MPC and requires it reach decisions by voting, to publish minutes, and to publish a quarterly report on (relevant aspects of) the economic outlook.

Proposition 1: Stay with a Lexicographic Objective in Primary Legislation

It also makes price stability – low and stable inflation – the MPC's overriding objective. In the jargon, the objective is lexicographic: the MPC can pursue its secondary objective only if the primary objective is fulfilled. Since the anchor needs constant reaffirmation given the political incentives to take risks with inflation, that is a good thing.

It says, for example, that when the risks to inflation are judged to be on the upside, the committee should act rather than sit on its hands, hoping that there will be benefits to real activity or jobs or labour participation or something else. Just that kind of gamble – running the economy 'hot' in pursuit of 'inclusive growth' – was, I suspect, at the heart of some of the mistakes committed during 2021 by the Federal Reserve, which has a so-called dual mandate. As Paul Volcker used to say, that makes no difference so long as one believes there is no long-term trade-off between price stability and economic activity (or, I would add, if one thinks stability is a necessary condition for long-run prosperity). But maybe the Fed had incentives to explore whether there was a trade-off in order to court public popularity, get reappointed or whatever.[6]

I would, therefore, stick with Britain's lexicographic objective.

Proposition 2: Clarify the Governance around Non-monetary Policy Balance Sheet Operations

The legislated regime does, however, suffer from a problem that, with hindsight, was neglected in the 1998 Act. It does not address inalienable central bank functions that do not fall to the MPC – most notably, acting as the monetary economy's lender of last resort (LOLR). In fact, although no other organ of British government is capable of acting as the LOLR because no other agency can print money, the Bank itself is not under any

---

[6] Arguing the Fed chair should have a single eight-year term, see Tucker (2021).

kind of duty to act as the LOLR. This came to head during the 2007 phase of the GFC.

The solution is to enact a legislative provision to the effect that the Bank should act as the LOLR wherever it judges stability to be threatened, subject to not lending to fundamentally bust firms.[7] Once the Bank was subject to that duty, Parliament could (and should) repeal the statutory power of the Treasury to direct the Bank to act as LOLR. That remedy, introduced in the 2012 reforming legislation, is the wrong way round: rather than clarifying what independence is for, it intrudes on monetary independence by creating space for tactical political considerations to shape LOLR decisions.

In addition – most certainly if that change were made but even if it is not – the Bank's LOLR and other non-monetary policy balance sheet operations should be placed under the formal control of an executive board (probably comprising the governor and deputy governors). At present, such powers are vested solely in the person of the Governor alone. That puts an awful lot of responsibility on one person and means that LOLR policy is not guaranteed to benefit from the kind of deliberation, among multiple points of view, that Parliament requires for monetary policy and, since 2012, for certain elements of stability policy.[8]

The Non-legally Binding Remit from the Treasury: One Thing to Keep but Some Important Changes

The legislated part of the UK's monetary regime includes an instruction to the Treasury to expand upon the MPC's mandate in a remit. The Remit itself is not legally binding and is not drafted like a legal norm (with terms defined, and so on). But it is treated by the Bank as part of the regime because plainly, under the UK's parliamentary system, the Executive could equip itself with statutory powers to issue a remit in a legally binding form.

---

[7] On the grounds for the constraint, see Tucker (2020).

[8] I recommended the proposed reform during 2012 and might usefully have made it public. The predicament arises because, except where legislation has bestowed specific powers on specific legal persons (e.g. monetary policy powers delegated to MPC), the powers of the Bank are vested in the Governor & Co., meaning the Court of Directors. The court has, for decades, chosen to delegate to the incumbent governor all the Bank's powers and responsibilities except those it expressly reserves for itself in a document called *Matters Reserved to Court*. Technically, court could remedy the problem by delegating to an executive board that it created under internal by-laws.

Proposition 3: Stick with Inflation Targeting

The first thing to say about the MPC Remit is that I would stick with inflation targeting, by which I mean the kind of flexible inflation targeting that has been in the Remit from the beginning in 1997.

One great merit of this is that anyone here in the hall can go home and explain to your friends or family why it is sensible to try to achieve low inflation. And you can also explain why the main instrument for achieving that is the interest rate since interest-rate changes turn up in people's savings rates (if they are lucky enough to have savings) and in borrowing rates. It is hard to overstate how much harder it was to explain money-aggregate targeting and its relatives. When, during the twenty odd years up to 2002, I was a staffer at the Bank, I was occasionally involved in writing papers on updating and applying monetary targets. So you set a target for the growth of some monetary aggregate of, let's say, 5%, and it turns out that it grows instead at 7%. But not infrequently, and sometimes accurately, the Treasury then wanted to say something like 'Don't worry, the old 5% is now 7% really because there has been a velocity shock, a shift in the demand for money.' Those words are, needless to say, gobbledegook to outsiders – meaning nearly everyone – and so amount to a kind of 'trust us' claim to indispensable but unmonitorable expertise. If, however, a series of (similarly signed) shocks to money-velocity come along, soon you are running out of compelling explanations for monetary targeting.

By contrast, it is easier to explain the effect on headline inflation of big cost shocks, such as from war-induced energy-price surges. Such explanations need, of course, to be accompanied by analyses of domestically generated inflation, in case it is also rising, but that is the core of the monetary policymaker's job. The very fact that people have been annoyed about inflation running well above target – in this country, in the US and parts of continental Europe – is evidence that that part of the inflation-targeting regime is working. It is as if the people are thinking something like 'They're meant to deliver inflation around 2%. They're not. What's going on? What's the explanation?' That is useful, and part of what the target system was meant to achieve: by incentivising the policymakers to analyse and explain what's going on and do something about any drift in domestically generated inflation.

Proposition 4: Prune the Remits Back to Where They Were in Spring 2013

The 1997 MPC Remit basically contained two propositions: an inflation target of 2% as the articulation of the legislation's mandate to maintain 'price stability' and an injunction not unnecessarily to amplify volatility in economic activity (and jobs) in the face of cost shocks. The constraint fitted with the statutory lexicographic scheme in the sense that the injunction had force only if medium-term inflation expectations were anchored to the 2% target.

All well and good. Well, except that there has been a tendency over relatively recent years, the last decade or so, to add things to the Remit. This is by no means confined to the MPC. The remit of the Financial Policy Committee (FPC) grew from roughly 4.5 pages in 2013, when the regime was formally established, to over 7.5 pages in 2021.[9] It then shrank back to around 5.5 pages in 2022 but retained the new emphasis on routinely getting on with supporting government policy so long as doing so does not damage stability. The MPC Remit has increased less but still in important ways.

For example, the 2013 version more or less instructed the MPC to introduce forward guidance. While it is certainly the case that the incoming governor wanted to introduce forward guidance, this came pretty close to HM Treasury telling the MPC how to do monetary policy (which greatly bothered some of my then colleagues).[10] Another addition was a longer specification of government economic policy, seeming to imply the MPC should be more active in providing support when it can. Others include some confusing comments about the governance of 'unconventional' operations and about monetary policy allowing inflation to deviate from target in order to accommodate FPC actions.[11]

This tendency to add to the Remits risks signalling a shift in the Treasury's conception of independence: no longer a mechanism for self-binding but more a means of pursuing government policy with insulation from blame. Whether or not that is intended, and it might not be, I propose that next year the Remit writer should, in their first internal draft, delete everything that has been added since 2012 and ask what they really need to add back. The Bank could usefully go through the same

---

[9] In word-count terms, this was a three-quarters increase, Aikman (2021). The FPC was modelled, broadly, but not completely, on the MPC: external members, an obligation to publish minutes, a requirement for HMT to issue a remit, and so on.

[10] Oddly, the (then) new Remit passage merely said that forward guidance was within the committee's discretion (properly, a question of law), and so was otiose except as a heavy hint. If the Remit had said anything, it should have been that a certain kind of forward guidance (see below main text) worked by inflation eventually, for a while, overshooting the target, and that that was OK with HMT.

[11] The former are confusing because a reader could infer that the MPC decides which assets the Bank can buy or lend against, but that is not so. The latter is at best incomplete because it does not cater for circumstances where the FPC needs to act partly because the MPC's policy is creating or fuelling imbalances or financial system vulnerabilities: the text says too much or too little.

exercise in order to work out how it feels about the expansion of the executive government's de facto expectations for the MPC and FPC.

Proposition 5: An Injunction to Explain, Qualitatively and Quantitatively, the Transmission of QE

Turning to economic substance, there are two things I would put into the MPC Remit that are not there at present. One of them concerns QE. I would not have guessed it, but it turns out to be useful to say that the MPC needs to explain – which means the individual members need to explain if they depart from a collective view – how QE works if and when they use it. One of the first things that the MPC did back in 1997/1998 was publish a document on their collective understanding of the monetary transmission mechanism. Individual members were not obliged to endorse it but they each did. By contrast, it has sometimes been quite hard to tell how MPC members think QE works, including crucially how potent (or not) they believe it is.[12]

At times, some members have subscribed to the portfolio-balance account, where QE affects term 'premia' (and perhaps other risk premia). But that explains merely why gilt purchases will affect the yield on gilts and close substitutes. One still needs to explain why compressing term 'premia' is expected to affect the path of aggregate demand.[13]

Some MPC members, rejecting that account of QE, have seemed to subscribe to the alternative signalling account, whereby QE reinforces the force of forward guidance that the policy rate will remain low for a long time. But if one holds to the signalling theory, then it is not obvious why one needs to do much QE at all. One could argue that 'throwing the kitchen sink at it' underlines the commitment, but that argument has force only if the 'sinks' in question have effects that reinforce credibility.

In other words, a signalling-theory advocate needs to explain the mechanism via which QE delivers the supposed signal. One possibility is the consequent exposure to financial losses, but that cuts both ways. And where that sub-account is rejected, as I believe some MPC members have, a substitute mechanism of some kind needs to be invoked. QE cannot be a signal just because someone, however authoritative, says it

---

[12] In 2021, the Bank reported that not much research had been conducted on QE since 2013. I understand that that has since changed (Bank of England, 2021).

[13] As former US FOMC member Jeremy Stein pointed out years ago, if term 'premia' are artificially compressed for a period, there is a risk-free arbitrage in borrowing long and investing in a default-free overnight instrument. That is not conducive to lower-term premia stimulating extra real investment. The point is not that the no-effect story is true but that policy-makers (not subscribing to the signalling account) need to explain why they *each* think it is not true.

is. If that alone were enough, the Governor waving from the steps of the Bank would suffice if they proclaimed it a credibility-affirming signal. In the transmission of monetary policy, hydraulics come before expectations.

As well as qualitative explanation, the policymakers' account of the transmission of QE needs to be quantified. As things stand, it is quite hard to discern when central banks – not only in Britain but also, I should stress, the US FOMC and so on – judge that they need more QE, how much they believe a bit more QE will affect the outlook for demand in a year or so and, given lags, for inflation some time after that. That is an uncomfortable gap because surely the policy committees need to form just that kind of quantitative view – an expectation subject to uncertainty – when, favouring more QE, they decide how much more to do.

So I think the Remit could usefully be revised to say, in effect, that we do not want to live with this gap and that, therefore, the MPC should fill it if (or whenever) it is going to use QE as an instrument of monetary policy. The importance of this is underlined when one remembers that QE, when massive and continued over a long period, effectively switches off the bond market's vital signals on credibility.

Proposition 6: Distinguish QE from Market Maker of Last Resort and Other Asset-Purchase Operations

The other thing I want to say about QE is that it is important to distinguish QE purchases of government bonds (and other instruments) from purchases that serve other purposes. QE is about stimulating aggregate demand in order to achieve the inflation target.

The gilt purchases in October 2022 were not badged as QE and rightly so because they were intended to stabilize the gilt market and to break the spiral of forced selling by highly levered pension funds (although see below). For not dissimilar reasons, while recognizing the terrible pressures created by the particular circumstances, I think it was a mistake to treat the spring 2020 purchases as QE, which meant not reversing them once market conditions had stabilized. That is because it was odd to think of stimulating aggregate demand when aggregate supply was closing down (voluntarily and by government order). Instead, the problem faced by governments (elected fiscal authorities) was how to get cash to households and small businesses. There was no need for central banks to finance that fiscal support once government bond markets were functioning and, in terms of the public finances, every reason not to do so given the precious opportunity to lock in extraordinarily low long-term yields (below the average of any plausible path of monetary policy rates).[14]

There was, by contrast, good reason for the Bank of England and, in the US, the Federal Reserve, and other central banks, to intervene to stabilize government bond markets during the exceptional volatility triggered by the realisation that Covid-19 was serious. But that would have been a market-making of last resort operation, which might not have needed to be anything like as big as the 'QE' purchases actually made, and which in any case would have been unwound, with bonds being sold back, avoiding the monetary overhang, once markets stabilized.

The key thing here is not that my judgement on those particular episodes is right; it is, rather, that I think the Remit should require the Bank to distinguish between different types of gilt (and other) purchase operations according to their purpose. Recently Steve Cecchetti and I published a piece in VoxEU identifying five purposes that a central bank could have in buying government bonds in the market.[15] They are, briefly, to stimulate aggregate demand (monetary policy); to provide emergency financing to government; to stabilize bond markets; to provide liquidity to those selling the bonds; to steer the allocation of credit to (or away from) particular destinations. Whether the last is legitimate for an independent central bank is moot (but not elaborated upon here).

In any case, each purpose needs its own mini-regime, as the second to fifth purposes are obviously not monetary policy as such (even when they help the transmission of monetary policy and can belong with the central bank). The label 'QE', and the governance it entails, should be used only when the purchases are designed directly to stimulate aggregate demand. Purchases for other purposes are not for the MPC to decide. That means, by the way, that any net injection of base money via non-MPC operations must either be formally approved at the time by MPC (making it a joint operation) or, alternatively, sterilized (or as the Bank used to say, drained). As it happens, that did not happen when, during October 2022, the Bank created money when conducting market-making of last resort operations to calm the spiralling effects on the gilt market of forced sales by highly levered and illiquid pension fund vehicles.[16]

---

[14] Tucker (2002).   [15] Cecchetti and Tucker (2021).

[16] Whenever the Bank is operating a regime of reserves averaging, the draining operation can occur any time before the end of the maintenance period (but has to be larger, the more the operation is delayed). When there is no maintenance period, as in recent years, sterilisation needs to be effected quickly so that the nature of the money injection is not mistaken for QE and so that the MPC's prerogatives are respected.

Proposition 7: Review the Remit for Coping at the Zero Lower Bound

The final thing I would say about the substance of the MPC Remit, and here I do not have an answer, is that once central banks have got through the current inflationary and stagflationary problems, as eventually they will, they might well find themselves again facing the problem of a low long-run equilibrium real rate of interest and therefore the problem of monetary policy hitting the zero lower bound (ZLB) (for nominal rates) more frequently than my generation of policymakers would have guessed. So what is to be done about that? Does it mean that there should be stronger automatic fiscal stabilisers or that there should be a higher inflation target, or both?

Half a decade or so ago, not a few people thought advanced economies, including the UK, should be reviewing that big challenge. It will still have to be addressed unless the forces reducing risk-free real interest rates go into reverse.[17]

It is anything but easy to judge how the monetary regime should be tweaked, however. For example, it would be awkward to raise the inflation target now because it would be done from a position of weakness. Had central bankers been onto the domestically generated inflationary pressures much more quickly, it might have been possible to use the separate cost-shock effects on headline inflation to raise the target opportunistically. But that wasn't to be. Instead, given the blows to credibility over the past couple of years, there is a tangible risk that raising the target now could simply fuel concerns the target might be raised still further if and when expedient in the future.[18]

The Appointments Process

As a bridge between remarks on the design of the regime (law and Remit) and the MPC's delegated stewardship of the regime, there is something to be said about the composition of the MPC, since obviously the stewards are flesh-and-blood men and women who have been appointed by the executive government to exercise the powers conferred by Parliament.

---

[17] The Fed did conduct a review but ended up with a new regime designed to cope only with the problem they then had (below target inflation while stuck at the ZLB). In particular, the new regime effectively precluded pre-emptive action in the face of inflationary shocks (to domestically generated inflation or expectations). I would say that a necessary criterion for any adequate regime is that it should be capable of addressing a wide range of plausible problems, including those prominent in the history of monetary policy.

[18] A point also made by former Fed chair Ben Bernanke in Wessel (2018).

Proposition 8: Put the Bank of England Back into the MPC

On this, it is, I suggest, instructive to make a contrast between, on the one hand, the composition of the MPC that I served as secretary and then joined as a member twenty-odd years ago with, on the other hand, that of the MPC over more recent years. The early MPC had, at the beginning, at least four or five members who were deeply versed in the territory where monetary theory meets monetary practice: in other words, in the questions that arise if you actually want to do QE, forward guidance, and so on. They were Eddie George, Mervyn King, Charles Goodhart, Ian Plenderleith and later myself. By the time Mervyn was Governor, I think that there were three, maybe three and a half people on the committee who fulfilled that criterion. But since Paul Fisher retired from the committee in the mid-teens, the number would be either zero or one. And that is the point of mentioning this. On the face of it, it looks like an environment where Eddie George, a great central banker, might not have got onto the MPC at all, let alone become Deputy Governor or Governor. That is because it is not easy to see how his particular skill set, from his years on the Bank staff, would have been valued sufficiently to get onto the committee.

So there is a serious point about the composition of the committee: about the skill sets (plural) that society wants, or needs, on the MPC. Of course, the country should want the committee to include academic macroeconomists coming out of the top university economics departments, and it should also want business economists and sometimes different kinds of academic economists who can challenge the macroeconomic and microeconomic thinking of the MPC and the staff. But maybe central bankers steeped in the markets and the implementation of policy, and in reading the conjuncture, might be useful too; certainly, private sector market experience is not a substitute.

I doubt there is a formal cure for this. For example, while it would in principle be attractive to create a central banking equivalent of the UK's successful Judicial Appointments Commission, I doubt there are enough monetary and central banking experts to serve on such a commission without relying too much at any particular time on a handful of recent senior Bank office holders. Instead, the court (if it continues), the parliamentary oversight committees and interested commentators need to be prepared to speak out.

Reforms to Stewardship of the Regime

My proposals on the Remit and the make-up of the MPC concern Treasury stewardship of the matters delegated by Parliament to it. Now

I turn to the MPC's (and, more generally, the Bank's) stewardship of matters delegated to them.

Proposition 9: Return to the Inflation Report

First of all, although this sounds trivial, the Bank should announce, soon, that it is going to return to naming its quarterly report the Inflation Report, rather than stick with the still relatively recent innovation of calling it the Monetary Policy Report. The point of returning to the Inflation Report is that it reminds everybody, including the committee themselves, and the Bank's staff, that there is a lexicographic objective, whereas the shift to Monetary Policy Report conjures, maybe even internally, something uncomfortably close to 'We've conquered this inflation stuff. It is anchored. What else can we do with our monetary policy instruments – to promote our idea of the good, or whatever the government wants?'

I do not want to get into the contents of the quarterly report; it now includes analysis of a special topic, which is a good thing but otherwise seems to carry less analysis of the standard data than a decade or so ago. I would suggest, however, that the Bank needs to re-emphasize that, even though not a sensible target, money matters (as an indicator and, on some views of risk premia, as a causal actor).[19] So the committee should include analysis of the monetary aggregates, not just credit quantities and prices, in its publications and policy statements. Although not of burning interest to many members of the public, this would tie the Bank to taking the monetary aggregates seriously and signal that to the commentators who intermediate between Bank publications and the wider public.

Proposition 10: Return to Staggered Announcements of Decisions and Forecasts

At the risk of sounding like the old TV programme All Our Yesterdays, I would also urge the Bank to move away from announcing the MPC's decision, the MPC minutes and the Inflation Report forecasts all at the same time. The current set-up, introduced about half a decade ago, imposed extraordinary time constraints. It is important that the discussions of the economic outlook and, separately, of policy are not impaired by having to think at the same time about how to write them up. Among

---

[19] In his 2022 Beesley lecture, John Vickers (chief economist of the Bank during the MPC's first few years) recorded that in August 1998 the *Inflation Report* had contained seven charts or tables about money, with roughly 50 mentions of money in the main text, whereas in August 2022 the numbers were, respectively, zero and one.

other things, having to make the policy decision, and write all the explanations, a day or so before the MPC formally makes and announces its policy decision might make it harder for the committee to take account of late news and arguments. It also forfeits the opportunity to ensure commentators devote time, separately, to the policy settings and decisions, to the minutes of the committee's deliberations (including minority votes), and to the committee's collective view of the outlook.

Proposition 11: Exercise Self-Restraint with Forward Guidance

Finally, I want to say a couple of things about forward guidance. First, it is vital to distinguish between, on the one hand, Woodfordian[20] forward guidance when policy rates are stuck at the ZLB and, on the other hand, statements about future policy when no longer stuck at the ZLB. That vital distinction – sometimes characterised as Odyssean versus Delphic – has been blurred, elided or just junked.[21]

In Woodfordian-Odyssean mode, the policymaker is trying to commit to keep policy rates low for too long; that is, beyond the point of economic recovery and a return of underlying inflation to (or above) target.[22] But the same sounds and scribbles – 'forward guidance' – have come to be habitually employed when, freed from the ZLB constraint, policymakers are merely talking about what they are going to do. The first is a commitment, the second a prediction, and so they obviously do not have anything like the same analytical grounding. The elision, moreover, is costly because policymakers' unqualified predictions about their future choices are unreliable, not for any nefarious reason but because they do not know what is going to happen in the world. They do not know which known risks will crystallize and which shocks will take them completely by surprise.

Policymakers talking about what they expect to do might help compress volatility on Wall Street or the City of London, but that is not the central

---

[20] After the economist Mike Woodford.

[21] The first use of those labels might have been in Campbell et al. (2012).

[22] The edict to keep the policy rate low for 'too long' captures the thought that the strategy is, technically, time inconsistent. That, in theory, is how it works: the expectation of (above-target) future inflation reduces real interest rates, which stimulates demand today etc. Woodford himself stipulated that the prescribed path for rates should depend partly on the future incidence of shocks. In practice, those who employed the strategy were gambling that once the 'too long' phase was reached, the economy would not be hit by a nasty cost shock that added to the domestically generated inflationary pressures from excess demand. That gamble did not pay off (the energy and supply-chain shocks). It is not clear how many commentators understood this gamble against the Gods before it went awry. Forward guidance perhaps worked in theory but not in practice.

mandate and so risks policymakers taking their eyes off what is actually going on in the economy and the balance of risks to demand and inflation over the years ahead.

The way I would sum up my prescription, then – for the ECB and Fed as well as Bank of England – is: talk less about yourselves, and instead talk more about the economy, about the economic outlook, with its uncertainties and risks.

Second, but not wholly separate from that first point, forward guidance (of either kind) cannot work unless there is a stable super-majority in the committee. If 'guidance' issued today for, say, the next five years is vulnerable to being dropped at the next meeting because just one member has changed her/his mind, and that possibility is understood, the initial 'guidance' will be given little weight. In particular, in practice Woodfordian guidance has to tie the hands of future members of the committee if it is to work; they effectively join with their votes pretty much decided for them in advance unless they want to overturn the apple cart.

In consequence, forward guidance provides another route for pushing a 'one person, one vote' committee towards a leadership-led committee. Here, I think there is a trade-off that needs to be recognised between the efficiency benefits of articulating a state-contingent plan for future policy and the costs of losing 'one person, one vote' (when people in the committee are truly free to say in any meeting, 'I really don't agree with that').

My view is that the (net) benefits of committee deliberation that culminates in a free vote exceed the costs of not conveying a collectively agreed future path for the policy rate. I concede that not doing the latter has some efficiency costs, but I think true 'one person, one vote' decision-making helps avoid big mistakes. In other words, I think avoiding big mistakes is more than worth epsilon sacrifices in efficiency. If it has the benefits I claim, that is because each member is accountable for their own vote and accordingly under a burden to explain it (including to themselves!).

I hope it is apparent why my first and second concerns about forward guidance are related. Briefly, one starts off needing a chair-led policy during Woodfordian (commitment) forward guidance, but that very different committee culture risks, through habit, becoming embedded by the time the ZLB problem has passed, and so of persisting during a period of predictive 'forward guidance'. Worse, if the first phase lasts many years, as it did, new members of the committee are not immediately inducted into a culture of individual decision-making and accountability.

If that sounds a bit abstract, ask yourself whether it is plausible that all (every single one) of the individual members of the MPC during its first couple of decades would have seen no risk to inflation during 2020 and 2021. It is the unanimity that is startling, and I suggest that is a product of the ultimately corrosive culture of forward guidance.

I do not quite see how to cater for this in the Remit from the Treasury, so instead I think it is a matter for the committee's stewardship. Recent minority votes, whatever one thinks of their merits or demerits, are encouraging in this respect. So is the MPC's move to discuss unlikely but plausible scenarios, which are a potentially useful tool for conveying its reaction function (so long as the analysis addresses circumstances in which the anchor has slipped or needs to be secured).

Proposition 12: MPC Should Be Relaxed about FPC Offsetting Some of the Risks to Stability from Long Periods of Easy Monetary Policy

Finally, and briefly, MPC should be relaxed if FPC chooses – as it should have done but did not – to offset some of the effects of persistently easy monetary policy on risks to financial stability. Many people worried that a combination of QE and forward guidance was fuelling a search for yield that, in time honoured ways, drove up leverage and liquidity mismatches outside the re-regulated banking sector. Short of a general policy for shadow banking and its ilk (a separate question), stability policymakers could usefully – I think, should – have increased minimum collateral requirements in traded markets and in clearing houses. That would indirectly have capped leverage in those markets.

The point here is that MPC should not worry if FPC does act in that kind of way to preserve stability. This seems to underline the value of introducing voting to FPC, which might help overcome a bias against action but belongs to a separate debate rather than to thoughts prompted by the MPC's twenty-fifth anniversary.

Summing Up

Inflation is always and everywhere a political economy problem. A nominal anchor can be achieved only through the design of regimes that are incentive compatible for elected politicians and unelected technocrats. It is no easy thing, as the key moving parts of any regime can be picked apart. After the unravelling of the Bretton Woods international monetary system half a century ago, it took Britain 25 years to find its way to a decent monetary regime. Now that regime is itself 25 years old and in recent years has been developed or expanded in various ways.

This chapter has set out a dozen propositions aimed at underpinning and, perhaps, revitalising Britain's MPC and the regime entrusted to it. It has not addressed the many reform proposals – such as merging the MPC and FPC or having regional representatives on the MPC – with which I disagree. Nor has it addressed the incentives of the regime's parliamentary and other overseers.

References

Aikman, David (2021), 'How has the Financial Policy Committee's objective changed since its inception?' *Macroprudential Matters*, 9 December.

Bank of England (2021), 'Evaluation of the Bank of England's approach to quantitative easing'. Independent Evaluation Office Report.

Campbell, Jeffrey R., Charlie L. Evans, Jonas D. M. Fisher, and Alejandro Justiniano (2012), 'Macroeconomic effects of Federal Reserve forward guidance', in Romer David and Justin Wolfers (eds.) Brookings Papers on Economic Activity, Spring. Brooking Institute Press, 1–80.

Powell, Jerome (2023), Sveriges Riksbank Panel on 'Central bank independence and the mandate – evolving views'. Federal Reserve Board, 10 January.

Steven, Cecchetti and Paul Tucker (2021), 'Understanding how central banks use their balance sheets: A critical categorisation'. 1 June VoxEU.org. Centre for Economic Policy Research.

Tucker, Paul (2002), 'Quantitative easing, monetary policy implementation, and the public finances'. *Institute for Fiscal Studies Green Budget* 2002, chapter 7.

Tucker, Paul (2018), *Unelected Power: The Quest for Legitimacy in Central Banking and the Regulatory State*. Princeton University Press.

Tucker, Paul (2020), 'Solvency as a fundamental constraint on LOLR policy for independent central banks: Principles, history, law', *Journal of Financial Crises*. 2(2), 1–33.

Tucker, Paul (2021), 'The fed appointments process should be overhauled', *Financial Times*, 23 November.

Wessel, David (2018), 'Alternatives to the Fed's 2 percent inflation target'. Brookings, 7 June, pp. 13, 17.

Annex: Details on the methodology for the classification of level of disagreement

For the Bank of England MPC and for the Federal Reserve FOMC, the classification of the level of disagreement was done based on publicly available voting information. For both central banks, we created four categories:

- Unanimity: when all members voted in favour of the policy decision;
- Overwhelming majority: when all members except one voted in favour of the policy decision;
- Strong majority: when the number of votes in favour of the policy decision was between overwhelming majority and majority;
- Majority: when half of the members plus one voted in favour of the policy decision.

For the ECB Governing Council, the classification of the level of disagreement was derived from information found on transcripts of press conferences following the Governing Council monetary policy meetings, which also include transcripts of the Q&A with journalists, and, since 2015, the accounts, that is, the summaries of the discussion of the monetary policy meetings published by the ECB. Exceptional press releases may also be considered. We followed the methodology and classification proposed in Claeys and Linta (2019), which has three categories that can be described as follows:

- Unanimity: all members of the Governing Council agree on the policy decision;
- Consensus: the policy decision is supported by the entire Governing Council, by some more enthusiastically than others, but this does not require a vote;
- Majority: some members disagree, and a vote might be needed.

Index

Printed in the United States
by Baker & Taylor Publisher Services